God Can Walk On His Eyeballs

The 10 Most Amazing Things

He Taught Me

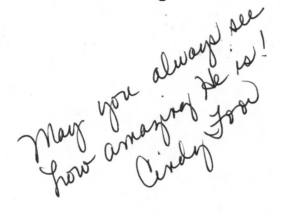

May you always see how amazing He is!

Cindy Foor

Cindy Foor

www.cindyfoor.com

Outskirts Press, Inc.
Denver, Colorado

Outskirts Press, Inc.
http://www.outskirtspress.com

ISBN: 978-1-59800-716-9

Outskirts Press and the "OP" logo are trademarks belonging to Outskirts Press, Inc.

PRINTED IN THE UNITED STATES OF AMERICA

Foreword

Cindy Lu Lingenfelter was THE "little girl, who had a little curl, right in the middle of her forehead. And when she was good, she was very, very good. But when she was bad, she was horrid." She has grown from a strong-willed child, to a rebellious teenager, to a self-confident young adult who could do everything on her own, to a young mother in the pit of depression, to a broken and surrendered child of God. She can now look back and see that the trials and consequences of her choices were all used to bring her to the place she is today – a humbled and obedient servant of her almighty Father.

As Cindy continues to seek God's will for her life and continues to work for Him, she is frequently under attack from the one who wants to thwart God's plans. She has been tested, and has relied on Jesus' promises to sustain her. Perseverance and a desire to please her Lord have resulted in this book you have picked up. Please allow the Holy Spirit to speak to you today through Cindy's writing. You will laugh, you will cry, you will see His hand in her life and in these lessons.

Although Cindy will quickly point out that I am "much older" than she is, I submit to her authority as a teacher. However, as her big sister, she is not the boss of me! I love you, Cindy, and I can't wait to see what God does next.

Shari (Lingenfelter) Duncan

Preface

It has been a deep desire of my heart for many years to write a book, yet life just seemed to keep happening to me and I allowed all kinds of things to prevent me from completing it. Until now.

In December 2005, while I was praying, I realized this was more than just a heart's desire – it was my calling from God. I was <u>called</u> to write, and my failure to finish this book was nothing less than disobedience toward God. I made many excuses and I became quite adept at explaining all the good reasons that I allowed other things to take priority over what God called me to do. But I made a plan and committed to God that I would make the time, and that I would be obedient to Him, no matter what. I took a leave of absence from work, and established a schedule to write from home. But some of "the best laid plans…"

Right after I began my leave of absence from work, one of the most peculiar, frightening things happened. I was driving home from a meeting at my church – a very familiar trip through back roads of York County, Pennsylvania. The meeting ended a bit later than I thought it would, so I called my husband, Steve, on my way home to be sure he wasn't worried about me. As I approached some railroad tracks that have been converted into a rail trail for walkers and cyclists, I noticed a car waiting to pull out from the parking area of the rail trail onto the main road. I slowed down for the railroad tracks and the car was directly to my right. Then it happened. It was so sudden, loud, and unexpected, I couldn't process it.

Still on the phone with Steve, I yelled, "I think someone in that car threw a rock at me!" It made me angry. As soon as I crossed the tracks, the car quickly fled the scene, in the opposite direction. I was alone on that dark country road and was a bit unnerved, so I kept Steve on the line and continued to drive until I was in a public, lighted location. I heard a strange popping noise toward the back seat of my car and I couldn't figure out what was causing it. When I stopped and got out of my car, I found the back panel window of the passenger side had a big hole in it, and the glass was crackling and shattering into what looked like a million little pieces.

Assuring Steve that I was ok, I hung up with him and dialed 911 to report the incident. They quickly dispatched an officer to the location where the incident occurred and sent another officer to assist me. He immediately recognized the hole in my window as the result of a pellet gun shot, not a rock. His words caused my emotions to shift from anger to fear. "This was not a rock, Ma'am. Someone shot at you."

He explained to me that a pellet gun could have been deadly, or at the very least it could have caused me to wreck my car. But the pellet went through the window only to hit a very small piece of metal behind it, which stopped the pellet from going anywhere else. The officer was a Christian, too, and his words I found comforting. "This," pointing at the metal behind the glass, "is the grace of God."

And the grace of God is sufficient for me! That's why today, as I finally BEGIN to FINISH this book that I truly believe God called me to write, is different. No more excuses. The enemy has no power or authority in my life. My heart belongs to Jesus Christ! And to Him, be all the glory!

My prayer for you is that you will find my words comforting – because someone else has "been there, done that!" Encouraging – because, with God's help, someone else has found her way through some tough things in this life. Humorous – because I truly believe that when the choices are laughing or crying, we should choose laughter as much as possible! And hopeful – because there is much joy in this life and Christ died that we might live it to the fullest! Praise God!

Thanks for giving my book a try! I'll be praying for you.

Introduction

Your curiosity most likely caused you to pick up this book. I'll bet you were wondering, "What in the world is *this* book about?" I mean with a title like **God Can Walk on His Eyeballs**, what are you supposed to think, right?

Well, before you turn more pages, please allow me to share with you the story behind my thinking. (I should warn you, though. Once you've taken a peek into how I think, you may become very frightened. Just ask my family and friends! Consider yourself forewarned.)

My husband, Steve, and I have two wonderful, beautiful children - Brittany, who, at the writing of this book, is 24, married to John, and mother to Brynn Elizabeth, our beautiful granddaughter. And Brandon, who is 21, a Corrections Officer at a local county prison, working on his degree in Criminal Justice, and engaged to his beautiful Lauren. Throughout my book, you will hear much about my children, my husband, my family and friends, because they are such an important part of my life, and also because, quite frankly, they are such wonderful sources of material!

This story involves my son, Brandon, when he was only 4 years old. At that age, most kids ask lots of questions – so many that they can drive their parents crazy. Brandon was no exception, except that when he had a question – or even just a statement to make – he always said, "I have two questions." (I believe he secretly hoped to keep my attention for longer than just what one question would require.)

Brandon and I were riding down the country road to my parents' home one day, just the two of us. Brandon was a thumb-sucker then and when he wasn't talking or busy playing, he was most likely sucking his thumb. He always had really good suction, too, because when he pulled his thumb out of his mouth, you could hear a "pop" from the release of suction. This was the case today.

Quietly, we drove down the road, when I heard it. "Pop!" And out came the thumb, followed by "Mommy, I have two questions."

"Yes, son, what are they?" I replied.

"Do you know who Batman is?" he asked.

"Yes, I know who Batman is. Why?"

"Is God better than Batman?"

"Oh, my yes! God is WAY better than Batman," I enthusiastically replied.

"WOW!" he exclaimed. (I could see that he was quite impressed with God.) And back into his mouth went his thumb.

There was silence for the next mile or so, then "Pop!" "Mommy, I have two questions again."

"Yes, son, what are your questions now?"

"Do you know who Superman is?"

"Yes, I know him, too."

"Is God stronger than Superman?"

"Oh, yes, Brandon. God is much stronger than Superman."

"WOW!" he said with even more enthusiasm than before as he returned his thumb to its favorite location.

At this point, I began to pray for wisdom. I wasn't sure where this conversation was going and I was a bit nervous about what might be asked of me next, I must confess. As I looked over at him, I could see the wheels turning in Brandon's head and I knew this conversation wasn't over. I knew there was more to come. I wasn't disappointed.

Soon, I heard it again. "Pop!" "Mommy?"

Before he had a chance to say the "two questions" line, I replied, "Yes, Brandon? Now what questions do you have?"

In his sweet little voice, he hesitatingly asked, "Can God walk on His eyeballs?"

I just looked at him a few times. His big bluish-green eyes eagerly awaiting my wise reply. But now, the wheels in MY head were turning! I tried to process this question, and prayed fervently for the right answer. Thankfully, I quickly came to the only one possible.....

"Yes, Brandon, if He wanted to, God COULD walk on His eyeballs!"

"WOW!!!!!!" He was so excited! He popped his thumb back into his mouth – he was completely satisfied with my answer. I could only smile and shake my head in amazement.

It was one of the most precious moments of my life as a mother. Our God is so very amazing! He can teach the heart of a four-year-old in a manner that even one that young can understand how truly amazing He is. And to top it all off, God allowed me the privilege of watching Him personally teach my little boy.

I was so excited! Brandon and I just sat there, riding along in the car, smiling and contemplating the awesome nature of God Almighty!

It is from this premise, this foundation, that I write this book. It is a compilation of experiences, stories, and lessons I've learned – some I'm still learning – of how wonderful and amazing our God truly is! To Him be all the glory.

Acknowledgements

Without the love and support of my husband, my children, my parents, my sisters, and my friends, this book would never have been published.

Thank you, Steve, from the bottom of my heart for allowing me the time I needed to finish it. Being the sole provider isn't easy, I'm sure, but without the time off work, I never would have been able to pull it all together. I appreciate your sacrifice so much and I love you dearly.

To Brittany and Brandon, thank you for allowing me the freedom to share from our lives so openly. Without question, you are gifts from God, indeed, and I will always count it a privilege to be your Mom.

To my parents, sisters, and friends, your prayers, support, and encouragement to "get 'er done!" was the push I needed to finally finish. Thanks for loving me and for believing in my calling.

To my Lord and Savior, Jesus Christ, without you, I was so very lost. With you, all things are possible. I count all things as loss compared to the surpassing greatness of knowing You. May my life always be a reflection of You.

The 10 Most Amazing Things He Taught Me
(So far!)

Chapter 1
"He's Been There All the Time"

Growing up on a small farm in rural Pennsylvania, the world seems very small. Communities are close-knit and self-sufficient, and there is little need to travel to the nearest city except for an occasional major purchase, a medical appointment, or back-to-school shopping.

I am one of five daughters born to Walter and Evelyn and was raised in a beautiful location in the mountains of Pennsylvania (near Altoona) called Morrison's Cove. In addition to their jobs, Dad and Mom also had a small farm where they raised some beef cattle. Of all my sisters, I was the one who hated going to the barn the most. (I just couldn't stand the smell! I still can't.) I learned pretty early on that I could get out of the barn work if I busied myself with housework instead. I'd much rather wash dishes, clean the bathtub, or sweep the porch than have to go up to the barn. With so many others at the barn, I usually got out of it.

Of these five girls, I was the middle child, and all that goes with that connotation applies to me. I can definitely be labeled "the strong-willed child," that's for sure! My mother used to tell people that I was like the little girl in that nursery rhyme. You know, the little girl with the curl in the middle of her forehead. Remember that one? "When she was good, she was very, very good, but when she was bad, she was horrid?" That was me! Mom used to say that she knew whatever I decided I was going to do, I'd be successful at it. So she just prayed that I'd choose to be something good, because if I chose to be a bank robber, for example, I'd be the best one around!

We went to church every Sunday and of course, we sat in the same pew each week. I can remember several Sundays getting pinched under my arm because I was picking on my younger sister, Lori. To me, Lori was such an easy target, but Mom was such a good pincher. She could pinch just enough that I knew she meant business, and all the time she was pinching, she'd be smiling so sweetly at me. (She was an expert!)

One Sunday in particular, I "acted up" and refused to relent my strong will to the authority of my parents. I knew that if I was taken out of the service, I'd be facing a spanking. And that's exactly what happened. I wasn't going willingly, though! I kicked and screamed and dragged my feet across the heat radiators along the interior wall of the church sanctuary as Mom lugged me out of the service. She was so mad! (And yes, I got my well-deserved spanking!) Then of all things, Mom made me come *back* into the service. Talk about being humbled!

My strong will and ability to work things out to my preference (also known as manipulation), became strong patterns in my life. As I grew older, the pattern became more prevalent and I learned to live my life *my* way, and only *my* way. Now, don't get me wrong. I wasn't a complete terror. I learned, for example, that in order to get what I wanted, I needed to be obedient to my parents, to complete my chores, etc. But for the most part, you probably could say that in my little world in that small farm community in Pennsylvania, I lived life *my* way.

I graduated from high school and married Steve shortly afterward. We moved to Washington DC area to begin our new life together and to find jobs. My strong will, drive, and work ethic were recognized by my employers as "quality values" and I moved up through the ranks relatively quickly. My strong-willed nature was considered something good now, and I tapped into it whenever necessary, thus embedding the pattern of "*my* way" even more deeply into my nature.

After six years in the DC area, Steve and I decided we were ready to start our family, but we preferred that I be an "at-home mom." We couldn't afford to stay in the DC area living on only one income, so we decided to move back to Pennsylvania and raise our children where we were raised, with our families nearby. We sold our house, relocated, and not long afterward, I became pregnant with Brittany – just as I planned.

After getting her through the first few months of colic, she was the best kid in the world! She was always so pleasant, and sweet, and happy! Then, a few years after Brittany's arrival, along came Brandon. He was such a good baby! No colic (thank the Lord) and he sucked his thumb, so putting him down to sleep was easy because he always found his own conveniently attached pacifier.

Life was good and we were about ready to send Brittany off to kindergarten when Steve decided to take a job offer about three hours away. This, however, was not in *my* plan. I had always thought my children would attend school where I attended; we'd raise the children with daily visits from grandparents, aunts, uncles, cousins. Moving three hours away didn't mesh with what I always thought my life would be. All of a sudden, it wasn't happening *my* way! This was a tough one for me, and just like being dragged out of church, I didn't go very willingly this time either.

Reluctantly, I said I'd support my husband's decision and we packed up and moved to Lancaster County, Pennsylvania. Although Steve's new job was located in York, Pennsylvania, I had always said I wouldn't live there – ever! But if I had to move, I'd live in nearby Lancaster so I could at least be near one of my sisters and her family there. (See how that works? "I'll go, but I'll go *my* way.")

The first eleven months in Lancaster was horrible. Nothing against Lancaster, it just wasn't where my heart was. And my heart was solely focused on me and what I wanted. We had sickness, financial problems due to the unforeseen increase in cost of living, and Steve worked long hours at his new job so we were really missing him. Someone broke into our car, shattering glass all over Brandon's car seat. The neighbors' children were trying to teach Brittany things we didn't want her to know about yet. Get the picture? It was not a happy time in life. I began to become deeply depressed and withdrew into a very, very small world of my own. It was dark.

On the outside, however, you'd never know I was depressed. I functioned as wife and mother very well when anyone else was around, but when Steve went to work, Brittany went to school, and Brandon went down for a nap, I went away in my mind. I began having very dark thoughts and even contemplated suicide. If it weren't for my loving husband and my beautiful children, I'm not sure what might have happened. I just couldn't do that to them – they deserved so much better.

I began to keep a journal during those dark months because I had to have some place to put my thoughts. I found that when I put them down on paper, I could sort through them a little better. At least they weren't swimming around in my head so much. Plus, I could literally close the book on what I wrote down that day, attempting to overcome the darkness.

God Can Walk On His Eyeballs

It was during this dark time in my life that God really got my attention. He sent some Christian women into my life who attended Bible study and had a weekly prayer group together. Their children were in the same kindergarten class with Brittany and without my knowledge, they were praying for me. (Apparently, I wasn't as good at hiding my struggle as I thought.)

They invited me and my children to one of their weekly Bible studies after kindergarten one day. I remember how nervous I was. Not because I was shy or unsocial. I was always the class clown, the loud one - never shy, never unsocial. But because I wasn't sure why they wanted <u>me</u> in their Bible study/prayer group. I'd been in church all of my life, but this was something new to me. After attending a few weeks with these women, I recognized that they had something I didn't have. They had problems and struggles just like I did, yet they seemed at peace, they had joy, they were content. I knew I desperately needed those things in my life, too, but I just didn't know where to find them.

One night, very late, I was doing laundry, washing dishes, and paying bills - because I never got these things done during the day due to my depressed state of mind. It was about 2am when I made a big decision. I knew all about Jesus Christ and I received Him and His gift of salvation when I was ten years old in my home church. I remember very well the day I went forward and asked Him to be my "Savior." But this time, in the wee hours of that particular night, I asked Him to be my "Lord."

You see, at age 10, I did receive my free gift from God – salvation from eternal separation from Him - but I had never fully relinquished the *control* of my life to Him. I was still trying to live life *my* way, rather than surrendering to *His* way. So finally, at age 30, I surrendered.

It was just God and me at this wonderful moment, "getting real." I was finally being honest with myself and was telling God everything. I reached up to heaven, outstretched my arms, and with tears streaming down my face, I cried, "I know you're there, Lord. Forgive me. I don't know how to do this thing called 'life' anymore. I've messed things up so badly. I can't do it *my* way – it doesn't work right. Please, please help me do it *Your* way. I give it all up to You. I surrender."

I felt a "warmth" come over me that I had never experienced before. I knew my prayer was heard and I knew my prayer was answered, "Yes!" It was a prayer that was in perfect alignment with His will for my life – that I would seek Him first and seek His will before my own. (The answer to that prayer is always "yes," by the way.)

What I learned that night was despite my strong will, despite my desire to live life *my* way, God was there all the time, just waiting for me to surrender. He was waiting patiently for me. What amazing love our Savior has to offer! What a fool I was to not give Him His rightful place as Lord of my life long ago!

I encourage you to take a minute right now and ask these important questions.

- "What am I waiting for?"

- "What is it that I haven't fully surrendered to God?"

- "What is it that He has been patiently waiting for me to surrender to Him?"

- "What have I been doing *my* way, that I should be doing *His* way?"

Be honest with yourself. Be honest with God. He already knows! What are you waiting for? Wave the white flag and surrender to Him. He's been there all the time – waiting for you, too.

"He lifted me out of the slimy pit, out of the mud and mire; He set my feet on a rock and gave me a firm place to stand."

Psalm 40:2 (New International Version)

Chapter 2

"Contentment Can Be Found in Chaos"

After living in Lancaster, Pennsylvania for a short eleven months, we moved three hours back home, near our parents. The cost of living was so much greater in Lancaster that we couldn't afford to live there unless I worked full-time. With the added expense of daycare for Brandon and after-school care for Brittany, we just weren't making it financially. And since our children were still very young (Brittany was 5 and Brandon was 2), we decided it was better to live in an area we could afford until Steve's job paid him more. So he worked out of town all week (in York) and came home on weekends (to the Altoona area).

It wasn't easy, I'll be honest. But it did have its advantages. If the kids and I wanted cereal for dinner, we had cereal. Mommy had the entire bed to herself, except for two nights during the week. One night Brittany slept with Mommy and the other was Brandon's night. And the weekends were wonderful! We celebrated Daddy being home all weekend long.

But despite our efforts to be optimistic and to be more financially stable, I had to pick up some part-time work to help make ends meet. I worked six different part-time jobs around the needs of the children and my household responsibilities. I worked a few hours several days per week for my mother, who was an insurance and real estate agent. Mom's office was located in the downstairs apartment of a building they owned, which made it convenient to take Brandon with me. He'd play for a few hours in the morning until he was hungry. I would feed him lunch and afterward, he'd take a nap in his sleeping bag in the bathtub of the apartment! (Adorable!) When he woke up, it was time to go pick up Brittany from school, which was just up the street. It really worked out very well.

Other jobs I took included babysitting a few children on occasion, typing papers for college students, and maintaining inventory records for a friend's local video rental store. I also began to work as a home party plan jewelry sales consultant, choosing my own schedule for jewelry shows. And finally, I was hired by my local bank to be a "secret shopper." (When I did my banking, I would conduct business at a different branch each week then report back to the bank management about the service I received.) I earned $5 for each evaluation!

Sometimes, the extra work I did earned our milk money that week. Sometimes, it made the difference to enable us to purchase new tires. Other times, Mommy's money paid for new coats and boots that winter. I knew that this season of life wouldn't last forever, yet I didn't want to simply get through it – simply survive it. I wanted to live it – enjoy it.

Some call it "happiness," but God doesn't call it that. God calls it "contentment." And quite honestly, it wasn't "happiness" I was really looking for anyway. I needed something much deeper, much more meaningful than that. Something I could cling to when the days were nuts; something I could stand on despite the crazy chaos of daily life. So during this busy, chaotic season of my life, for the first time I embarked on a journey to seek God's perspective on this thing He calls "contentment." I wanted to learn to do this His way, so I went right to His source – His Word.

The Apostle Paul wrote much about contentment, but these were the verses I found first – in the Book of Philippians, chapter 4.

Paul is writing to the believers in Philippi to thank them for the gift they had sent to him upon learning of his imprisonment at Rome. He makes use of this occasion to report on his own circumstances, and to encourage the believers in Philippi to stand firm in their faith, regardless of persecution or difficulty.

In verses 11-13 he writes, *"I am not saying this because I am in need, for I have learned to be content whatever the circumstances. I know what it is to have plenty. I have learned the secret of being content in any and every situation, whether well fed or hungry, whether living in plenty or in want. I can do everything through Him who gives me strength."*

(New International Version)

Paul is very clear to say in verse 11 that he has *learned* to be content. I was so relieved to read that. Learning is a process; something that is taught, that needs to be understood, and then practiced. Paul had to learn how to be content. If Paul had to learn it, I could learn it!

Teaching involves effort on both the part of the teacher and of the learner. Each one has work to do. Without the wise instruction and patience of the teacher, success is limited. And without the willingness and interest on the part of the learner, success is almost non-existent. God is my teacher, through the Holy Spirit, and I am the learner. Paul also says here that he's learned to be content whatever the circumstances. The real questions for me were, "Am I willing to learn how to be content, no matter what happens in my day? No matter what happens in my lifetime?" I needed to decide if I would trust God to teach me how to be content, regardless of my circumstances.

Did you ever wonder why God allows difficult circumstances into your life? I certainly have! Paul did, too. In fact, he asked the Lord to remove some circumstances that were particularly tough for him.

In 2 Corinthians 12:7-10 Paul writes, *"To keep me from becoming conceited because of these surpassingly great revelations, there was given to me a thorn in my flesh, a messenger of Satan, to torment me. Three times I pleaded with the Lord to take it away from me. But He said to me, 'My grace is sufficient for you, for my power is made perfect in weakness.' Therefore, I will boast all the more gladly about my weaknesses, so that Christ's power may rest on me. That is why, for Christ's sake, I delight in weaknesses, in insults, in hardships, in persecutions, in difficulties. For when I am weak, then I am strong."*

(New International Version)

Paul asked the Lord to take his "thorn" of circumstances out of his life. In fact, three times he *pleaded* with the Lord to remove it. But what was God's answer? (I'm paraphrasing here.) "No, Paul. I won't remove it. You see, My grace is sufficient for you. My grace is all you need. Because I have allowed this thorn to remain in your life, you are weakened so you can rely on My strength, which is perfected in your weakness."

I looked at that passage over and over again. There were many difficult circumstances that God allowed to remain in my life – circumstances that weakened me severely. In my Bible, I wrote my name in verse 9, between the words "you" and "for" so my version now reads, "My grace is sufficient for you, _Cindy_, for my power is made perfect in weakness."

A few years after God taught me about the correlation between my weakness and His sufficient grace, He tested me about what I learned. (He'll do that, you know. He tests His children not because He needs to know if we learned it, but because *we* need to know if we learned it! But He also tests His children to give us the opportunity to please Him, to be obedient to Him through the test.) During this particular test, Steve and I experienced one of the most difficult periods of our life, where the circumstances were very difficult and very much out of our control.

Over the next three years, we experienced the following: (Hang in there with me, ok? It's a bumpy ride!)

We discovered a lump in my breast that was highly questionable, which resulted in many doctors' appointments and tests. Steve lost his job due to downsizing, so we relocated our family for his new job. The house we vacated did not sell for over a year. We finally sold the house, but our buyers wanted to rent it for a year to get their finances in order. After the year of renting our house, the buyers backed out at the last minute, leaving us with a dirty, unkempt home to clean and repair. Steve had a new job offer in that area, so we packed up to move back into our home that never sold. Steve had a heart attack the night before he was to meet with the new employer to finalize the paperwork for this new job. (He was only 41.) After recovery from the heart attack and subsequent surgery, Steve's new employer wouldn't return his calls. Since we already relocated the family back to our house, Steve returned to his former job, and we lived separately during the week and saw each other on weekends – for the second time in our lives. Nearly a year later, Steve's company eliminated his position. Finally, Steve landed another job near us, but before we could finish celebrating, the very next day I lost my job due to company purchase/merger.

Please remember that all of this happened in a short three-year period of time – job losses, relocations, health issues for both of us, financial stresses, not to mention the effects on our children from all of these changes, including new schools, churches, friends, etc. We did not have any idea what was going on! "Chaos" was a standard way of life for us during that period of time. And you must know that we were often on our knees, wondering why, asking God to make things better, and asking Him to remove our thorns. And you know, to this day, we don't understand what in the world God was doing through some of those things. We might never fully understand.

But this we do know - God's grace was sufficient! It's all we really needed. We depended on Him completely because we had to. There was no way we could have fixed this stuff on our own. It was completely out of our control. We became so weak in these circumstances that we needed Him and His provision like we never needed it before. And He was faithful! We never lost our home, we never missed a meal, and our kids transitioned just fine (at least we think so!). God's holy power was made perfect when we were weakened by some lousy circumstances.

Amazing, absolutely amazing! Only our God works that way!

Through these difficult years, God was showing me that my circumstances in life really can be divided into two categories: Circumstances over which I have control; and circumstances over which I have <u>no</u> control. Think about it – it's true.

For example, when Steve lost his jobs due to downsizing, he had no control over the decisions that were made about which positions were cut. And I didn't do anything wrong that caused a lump in my breast to appear. But if Steve had lost a job due to failure to comply with a company policy, or stealing from his employer, for example, then his circumstances would definitely be within the confines of his control, right?

I learned that God wanted me to evaluate my life to see if I was doing something I shouldn't be doing - or *not* doing something I *should* be doing – that resulted in my difficult circumstances. (It's called "sin.") The book of Jeremiah teaches that I cannot know my own heart, only God can. So in order to properly evaluate my own sin, I had to seek God's help, through the Holy Spirit. Then I had to deal with what I discovered. I had to confess it to God, seek His forgiveness, and turn away from it. I read in 1 John that God says He is faithful to forgive me and cleanse me from all unrighteousness. Oh, how I needed that promise!

But once I really evaluated my heart – which I could only do through the Holy Spirit showing me – and I dealt biblically with the sin I discovered, the difficult circumstances that remained were circumstances that were *not* under my control at all. These circumstances can be called "thorns."

And as Paul did three times, it's absolutely fine to ask God (even to *plead* with Him) to remove those thorns from your life. And sometimes, He will! Do you remember the lump I found in my breast? After countless doctors' appointments and tests, we scheduled a lumpectomy to have it removed. I was prepped for surgery, wearing a lovely hospital gown, IV in my arm, and technicians were taking one last sonogram picture of the lump to ensure accuracy of its location. After a few minutes, the technician came over to me and said, "Please wait for a minute, Mrs. Foor. We have to check with the doctor about something." I told her, "I realize that you can't tell me what's going on, but I want you to know that I'm choosing to believe the best in this situation." The radiologist consulted with my surgeon, and my surgeon came over to me with the final update. With a tear in his eye he said, "I just can't explain it, Mrs. Foor. The lump has completely disappeared!" I replied, "Who can explain our God? Looks like someone's not having surgery today after all!" Praise God!

But the other "thorns" that remained – the circumstances over which I had no control – the circumstances that I pleaded with God to remove, but they were still there – I knew what God said about them. He said *(and I paraphrase again)*, ***"No, I will not remove those thorns, Cindy. I will allow them to remain. Yet, know that my grace is sufficient to see you through this. My power will be*** *made perfect in your life because these thorns make you depend on Me. Trust me. I know what I'm doing."*

"Thorns" are sovereignly designed by God Himself, uniquely for my life. He has purpose in allowing them to remain, even if they're horribly painful. "Thorns" do not enter into the life of God's children without passing through the hand of God's permission first. He knew exactly what was coming my way, yet He permitted it.

Now, here's where the "why?" question usually enters my head. I can get stuck here, too, if I'm not careful. Asking the question, "why?" just means that I don't trust God's sovereign work in my life. That I don't think He really knows what He's doing. That He looked away for a minute and didn't notice that I'm nearly drowning with this one. That one slipped through His fingers directly into my life?

No way! No way! No way!

This was a tough one for me. Does God have the right to choose my circumstances – which "thorns" to allow to remain, and which ones to remove? Does He have the right to allow my thorn to remain, yet remove the same type of thorn from someone else's life?

Yes, of course He does – just because He is God Almighty. He created me. When I received Him as Savior, I became His child. He "purchased" me with His shed blood on the cross. He knows all about me. He knows my past, my present, and my future. He knows all about my circumstances. And He loves me more than I could ever fathom.

So why would He allow this type of tough love? Why would He allow difficult circumstances to remain in my life? The answer, I believe, is found in Romans 8:28-29.

"And we know that in all things God works for the good of those who love Him, who have been called according to His purpose. For those God foreknew He also predestined to be conformed to

the likeness of His Son, that He might be the firstborn among many brothers."

(New International Version)

In these verses, I learned that God promises His children who are obedient to Him (for this is how we show our love to the Lord according to John 14:15), that He will use our circumstances to conform us to the likeness of His Son. Think about that for a moment. To conform – to make us more consistent with – to be more like Jesus! Really consider what a privilege "thorns" can be! If God were to remove all of the thorns from our lives, we would never really be able to understand or to grasp the true meaning of His wonderful grace.

When I realized this, I looked back at the lousy circumstances I struggled through, especially during those three tough years. I could come to only one conclusion: If I could trade not having the "thorns" at all, versus going through the trials and coming out on the other side looking more like Jesus, I can truly say, "Thank you, Lord, for the trials. It was so hard, and I don't fully understand, but I know You were there all along. And I now have a better understanding of who You are, and I am more like Jesus!" Considering this great truth, for me, there is no trade.

One final thought about contentment. This last piece of the puzzle was a big one for me. Look at Philippians 4 again, specifically verses 12-13.

"I know what it is to be in need, and I know what it is to have plenty. I have learned the secret of being content in any and every situation, whether well fed or hungry, whether living in plenty or in want. I can do everything through Him who gives me strength."

(New International Version)

What exactly does Paul say is the "secret" to contentment? (see verse 13) *"I can do everything through Him who gives me strength."* The Good News Testament says it this way - *"I have the strength to face all conditions by the power that Christ gives me."*

Jesus Christ, Himself, is the "secret." I cannot tell you how excited I was to see the word "secret" in scripture! Here I was, searching God's Word for how I could find and get hold of this thing called "contentment," and He just put it right in there for me to see – as plain as day! The secret to contentment is Jesus! How wonderfully simple God made it for me to find and understand.

Can *you* find contentment in the chaos of your life? Regardless of your circumstances, my dear friends, if you have received Jesus Christ as your Savior, you do have the strength to face all circumstances. You don't have to try to be strong enough to endure it, or be powerful enough to overcome it – it is *His* strength and *His* power that will see you through. You don't have to be in control over everything, because He is in control!

Praise God! Thank you, Jesus! What an amazing Savior!

Chapter 3
"God Really is Faithful"

As I think back over my life, I know that I have been greatly blessed and God always provided for all my needs and the needs of my family. His track record of faithfulness is truly amazing! But there were many times that we were really struggling financially. It should be no surprise that it was during the times of financial struggle that we learned the most about God's faithfulness and His ability to provide for us.

One time in particular that comes to mind is when Steve was working out of town during the week and the kids and I "held down the fort" at home. (I think it's hilarious that I have to tell stories according to the time frame of where we were living – Washington, DC, Altoona, Lancaster, Altoona again, York, Altoona again, York again! It's ridiculous, isn't it?) Anyway, the *second* time we lived near Altoona, Brittany was in her early elementary years and

Brandon was in his preschool years. (Does that help?) I was working those six part-time jobs I mentioned earlier and was busy taking care of the house and raising our wonderful children. Those years were very "lean."

Brittany tried to pour a glass of milk for herself but she accidentally dropped the milk container onto the kitchen floor. We lost our milk supply for that week. She was so upset because she knew that was the only milk we had, and Mommy didn't have any more money until payday. So when we said our bedtime prayers that night, we addressed her concerns directly to God. As we prayed together, we told God we knew He saw what happened and we trusted Him to take care of us. We said, "Amen," and she went to sleep. To be honest, I had no idea how God would answer that prayer, but I knew He was faithful to His promises and to His Word.

After making sure the kids were asleep for the night, I went back downstairs to tidy up a bit. In my kitchen stood my Aunt Lorraine, holding her dog, JoSai. (Pronounced Jo-Say.) I had forgotten that I promised to dog-sit JoSai while Aunt Lorraine and Uncle Terry went out of town for a few days. I received all of the puppy-care instructions and kissed Aunt Lorraine good-bye. Before she went out the door, Aunt Lorraine told me she put the rest of *her* milk in my refrigerator because she was worried the milk wouldn't stay fresh until they returned. "I hope you can use it," she said.

I opened the door of the refrigerator and there it was – God's answer to Brittany's prayer - His provision – in a jug of milk, no less! Of course, Aunt Lorraine and I both cried as I told her the events of earlier that evening. Isn't He amazing?

The next morning, Brittany got up as I was preparing her breakfast. She opened the door of the refrigerator to get some juice and saw the milk. She jumped up and down, yelling, "Mommy! Jesus came here last night! Jesus came here last night!"

God Can Walk On His Eyeballs

Our God cares about every single detail of the lives of His children. He doesn't miss a trick. Don't you think for one minute that He doesn't see your tears, that He is ignoring your cries for help, that He doesn't know what you're going through, that he missed it when your milk was spilled out all over the floor. If He can deliver a fresh supply directly to my refrigerator the very night we asked for it, He can do anything!

God has demonstrated and proven His faithfulness to me and to my family in countless ways over the years. I don't have enough pages available in this book to share all of the stories. (I guess I'll have to write another book!) But the scripture verse that impressed me the most at that time of learning about His faithfulness is 2 Timothy 2:13 which says, *"If we are faithless, He will remain faithful, for he cannot disown Himself."*

(New International Version)

He was always faithful to me, that's for sure. In fact, cannot think of one time that God was not faithful, because just as the scripture says He cannot be anything but faithful – it's who He is! But what jumped out at me from that verse was the very first part – *"If we are faithless."* Even when I lose faith, He will remain faithful to me.

Did you ever "lose faith?" Do you ever have trouble trusting Him? Who hasn't? Who doesn't? I certainly have. I still do at times. You see, while God has clearly demonstrated His great faithfulness to me in countless ways all throughout my life, I still struggle at times with my faith in Him. Why is this so? What more do I need to see from Him? He's always done His part – He is always faithful. But what about my part of this relationship – what about *my* faith?

As God was teaching me about having faith and I was learning how to trust Him more, I found this great story that helped me define what faith really is. (I wish I knew who to credit for the story, but unfortunately I do not.)

Cindy Foor

There was a man who walked a tight rope across Niagara Falls. Many people watched him do it. To them, he asked, "Do you believe I can walk a tight rope across the Falls?" They all replied, "Yes," because they had just seen him do it.

Then, he pushed a wheel barrow on the tight rope across Niagara Falls. When he completed the feat, he asked the onlookers, "Do you believe I can walk a tight rope across the Falls pushing a wheel barrow?" To that they replied unanimously, "Yes." They had seen him do that, too.

Finally, a buddy of the tight rope walker climbed into the wheel barrow and the tight rope walker pushed him – in the wheel barrow – across the Falls!

When they finished, the tight rope walker asked the crowd, "Do you believe I can walk a tight rope across the Falls pushing a wheel barrow with a person in it?" "Yes!" they all exclaimed. For they were now believers in this guy's awesome abilities. They had, after all, seen him do it.

Then he looked at the crowd and asked, "Who's next?"

There is a difference between belief and faith. There is a difference between just believing what you can *see* – what the evidence shows or proves – and getting into that wheel barrow, isn't there? Faith is *belief* put into *action*. Faith is more than intellectually believing in something - it's getting *into* that wheel barrow!

This is the same kind of faith the Centurion Roman soldier demonstrated when he said to Jesus, **"But say the word, and my servant will be healed."**

(Luke 7:7 New International Version)

This soldier knew that all Jesus had to do was "say the word" and his servant would be healed from a terrible illness. This soldier understood that all that was truly necessary was to take God at His Word – to believe what He says and to act upon that belief. Just because God says so, it *is* so. (We used to sing a song when we were kids – "God said, I believe it, that settles it!" I love that song!)

That's how I want to live my life. I want to put my complete trust in what God says and know that it is completely, perfectly, accurately, beyond the shadow of any doubt – TRUE! There are too many unknowns in this world and life is full of too many questions. I want to live my life knowing the absolutes – God loves me, God is in control, God can do anything, God wants what's best for me, God knows exactly what He's doing, God's timing is perfect, His Word is truth. For me, this meant the difference between surviving my life and actually living it!

How are you doing with taking God at His Word?

- Just because HE says so......you believe Him?

- Just because HE says so......you really *are* loved?

- Just because HE says so......the impossible really can happen?

- Just because HE says so......you *can* be obedient to Him?

Here's the thing I had to learn about having complete faith in Him and in His Word - it doesn't have anything to do with me, really. It has everything to do with <u>Him</u>. It's the <u>object</u> of faith that makes the difference. If I put my faith in myself ("believe in yourself"), then what's possible for me depends solely on me. Hey, I've "been there, done that already." It doesn't work!

So how can I have faith that moves mountains? I can put my trust in the only One who can move mountains! Because with God, nothing is impossible. Whether I trust Him or not, He's still capable. Whether I believe Him or not, it is still so. My focus must be on the object of my faith, Jesus Christ, who, scripture says, is the author and perfecter of my faith.

There was a woman named Florence Chadwick who, in 1952, attempted to swim the 26 miles between Catalina Island and the California coastline. After about 15 hours of swimming, a thick fog set in and Florence began to doubt her ability to finish. She told her mother, who was in one of the boats accompanying her swim, she didn't think she could make it. She swam for another hour before asking to be pulled out. As she sat in the boat, she found out she had stopped swimming just one mile away from her destination. She couldn't see her goal. She said all she could see was the fog.

Putting faith into anything or anyone other than Jesus Christ will only take you so far. The Lord Jesus Christ is the only One who defeated death. He is the only One who has been given all authority over heaven and earth. And Jesus Christ is the only way, the truth, and the life. He must be the object of your faith in order for your faith to work.

Take Him at His Word, stop focusing on the fog, and get into that wheelbarrow, my friend! Trust Him to carry you over the "falls" of life because He's the only One who knows exactly what He's doing!

Great is His amazing faithfulness!

Chapter 4

"Who I Am in Christ is My True Identity"

To some people, I'm known as Steve's wife. To others, I'm Brittany's and Brandon's mom, or I'm Brynn's Nana, John's mother-in-law, or Lauren's soon-to-be mother-in-law (I made that one up). I'm also Walt and Evelyn's "third daughter."

(Brief sidebar -- Our parents often introduce their daughters by our number in birth order. For example, Debbie is number one, Shari is number two, Cindy is number three, Lori is number four, and Amy is number five. Dad has a great – and sometimes warped - sense of humor, so he often adds a bit more information. "Cindy's my third daughter to my first wife," he'll say. He always gets such confused reactions when he does this, which is his goal, of course! Just so you know, my mother (Evelyn) *is* Dad's first wife – she's his *only* wife! Dad just likes messing with people's heads.)

Cindy Foor

I am also a proud member of Grace Fellowship Church in York, Pennsylvania. I am the former Assistant Director of Women's Ministries there. I am a former Human Resources Manager in the corporate world. I am best friends with Tootie, Netter, Nanette, Kimmie, Wosie, Constance, Susie, and Teener, just to name a few. (You can't see me now, but I'm laughing at the thought of you sitting there, reading these names, and wondering, "What in the world? They sound like cartoon characters from the 1940's!") These gals know who they are. I have a tendency to nickname those closest to me.

So what's my point? Our identities - who we are - is usually defined by our relationships, our positions, our placements in life. And often these identities are good, meaningful, and valuable. But there have been times when my identity was short-circuited. The connection was not good.

When I battled depression, for example, my identity was all wrapped up in being a failure - a failure as a wife, as a mother, as a daughter, as a friend. You name it. All I could see was how I failed. A label I wore so well was "sinner." I was acutely aware of how much sin I committed against God and against others. I was not thin enough, not educated enough, not knowledgeable enough.

Why are we so quick to pick up labels like these? Why are they so easy to wear? Because we don't know who we really are.

I remember when I realized that I was missing this crucial piece of information. It was almost like I was looking at a jigsaw puzzle of my own face, but there were vital pieces missing. You know, the eyes, the smile, etc. I knew it was me because I could see enough to recognize my hair and skin tone, but part of me was missing – the part that made me, "me." The picture wasn't complete. I was having an "identity crisis."

A dear friend of mine, who greatly influenced my spiritual walk asked me, "Cindy, you don't know who you are in Christ, do you?"

24

God Can Walk On His Eyeballs

I replied, "I don't even understand that question, Joan. So no, I guess I don't know 'who I am in Christ.' What does that mean?"

She opened the pages of her Bible and led me to several passages, starting in Ephesians. (She just loves the book of Ephesians!) She had me read through the first chapter in Ephesians where I discovered I was chosen by God before the creation of the world; I was adopted as His child through Jesus Christ; through Him, I have redemption and forgiveness of my sins; and I am considered by God as a saint with a glorious inheritance. I continued to read through the next chapter in Ephesians and learned I have a seat in the heavenly realms with Christ, and through Christ I have direct access to the Father by one Spirit.

Joan told me to skip to Colossians, chapter 3, which says my life is hidden with Christ in God and when Christ appears, I will also appear with Him in glory. Verse after verse, I read through the scriptures, many of which I had read many times before. But this time, for the first time, I read them from God's perspective about how He sees _me_.

In the following days, I found countless verses that said I was God's child, I was bought with a price, I belonged to God, I was wonderfully made, I was dearly loved. The missing pieces of the puzzle were beginning to fit and the picture of my true identity was getting more and more clear to me. I had failed at many things in life, but God didn't call me a "failure." I had sinned and I continue to sin, but God says I'm a saint who sometimes sins.

For the first time in my life, I began to understand who I really am in Christ, and it made the world of difference to how I viewed myself, my life, and my purpose. I was reminded in 2 Corinthians 5 that, when I received Christ, I became a new creation; the old was gone, the new has come. I was reconciled back to God through Jesus.

I wondered, "How could I have missed such important information? I've been in church nearly all of my life, I've been doing detailed Bible studies for several years now – why did I not get this before?" Because I have a vicious enemy who lies to me. Lies are his best weaponry. His best (or worst) lies are aimed where he can harm God's children the most.

I struggled with knowing my real identity and was all wrapped up in my sinfulness. I began to believe I was a failure, I was worthless, and my family would have been better off without me. The enemy would whisper in my ear things like, "You know you're just a loser. No one really loves you - how could they? You'll just let them down as you always do. You can't be a good mother because you don't know what you're doing. And forget about being a good wife – you blew that a long time ago."

If you listen to lies long enough, eventually they will take root in your mind. Soon you'll begin to believe the lies in the very depths of your soul, and if you believe something long enough, it eventually becomes your reality. During all those years of depression, I was ensnared in the enemy's trap of lies and deceit and I didn't even know it. I desperately needed to replace those lies with the truth of who I was <u>in Christ</u>. I needed to renew my mind.

There's an old saying, "What you feed grows – what you starve dies." I knew I needed to feed the truth and starve the lies.

Brandon always wanted us to buy him a baby lion or tiger cub. He was fascinated with how cute they were and thought it would be such fun to play with one and even keep one in his room. He said, "I'll take care of it, Mom. You won't need to do anything."

"Yeah, right! Like that's gonna happen, son!"

Those baby cubs are so cute, though, aren't they? I mean, look at those eyes, those little ears, those adorable paws. They play just like kittens do. Oh, and have you ever seen a white tiger cub? They're the cutest, in Brandon's opinion. Oh my stars! Those gorgeous blue eyes!

But what happens to those cute adorable cubs? They grow up. They grow very large teeth and very sharp claws. Their legs grow strong, which enable them to run extremely fast. Their instinct is to track down their food. They kill.

"Be self-controlled and alert. Your enemy the devil prowls around like a roaring lion looking for someone to devour."

(1 Peter 5:8 New International Version)

"What you feed grows – what you starve dies. Feed the truth – starve the lies.

I have had considerable experience working in women's ministries and have counseled many women, both through ministry and in the workplace. In my experience, women struggle more with identity than anything else. We are all wrapped up in what we don't do, or what we should do, or pleasing someone else. We don't think we are worthy of anything good, and we have a hard time believing that we are truly lovable. We believe lies.

So how do we feed the truth?

We get into the Word of God and read it, we speak it, we meditate on it, we memorize it, and we hide it in our hearts. It's life-giving, life-altering, food for the soul. The Word of God is truth, and as Jesus Himself said, *"The truth will set you free."*

(John 8:32 New International Version)

If you're not sure about your real identity or if you've been believing the lies of the enemy, I strongly encourage you to take some time to look up some scripture verses about who you really are. Start in Ephesians and try Colossians next. Underscore or jot down the verses that speak to your heart. Then look at the book of John. You'll see a great picture of your Savior there. John will help you understand the Son's relationship with the Father and your relationship with Him. If Jesus Christ is your personal Savior, the book of John says that you are "in Him" and He is "in you."

While you very well may be someone's wife, the mother of several children, the daughter of wonderful parents, and you may hold a position of high importance, your real identity is not in those facets of your life. Your real identity is wrapped up, safe and sound in the most important relationship of your life – your relationship with God, through Jesus.

Who you are "in Christ" is the identification you should carry around in your wallet! Your identity is not in *who* you are – it's in *whose* you are. If you belong to Jesus, you're His! Start to look at it from His perspective! You are dearly loved by an amazing God!

Chapter 5
"Laughter is Good Medicine"

I have a really weird sense of humor – some call it "twisted." I think it's a gene I inherited from both sides of my family. I already mentioned my Dad's sense of humor, but my Mom can be fuuny, too. (Sometimes she doesn't even know she's funny, though!) Mom has always had a great appreciation for funny people – it's most likely one of the main things that attracted her to Dad. But Mom's gene pool is rich in humor, as well. Her Daddy, my Pappy, was one of the funniest people I've ever known. But with Pappy, his genes had a "piggyback" gene I call "ornery."

Do you know what "ornery" is? Perhaps it's just a regional term, I don't know for sure. Most people associate the word with someone who is cantankerous or irritable. But the negative connotation of the word is not how I see it. Please allow give you my definition of "ornery."

Cindy Foor

"Ornery" is an inherited gene (definitely dominant gene) that is often reflected through the eyes of the beholder. (In less scientific terms, you can see "ornery" in the eyes!) Carriers of this gene will pass it on to the next generation – it does not skip any generations. The main characteristics of an ornery carrier are tendency to poke fun at others, pick on others, and the ability to absorb the same treatment if reciprocated. (In fact, reciprocation is often invited and always welcomed.)

Pappy had the ornery gene, and I have the ornery gene, so that means my mother has it, too! (It doesn't skip generations, remember?) And now, I'm proud to say, my children have it and even our granddaughter has demonstrated great ornery tendencies at her young age of two!

Well, all of this to tell you that, while I have inherited a good sense of humor and orneriness, I also often choose to see things in life from a "funny" perspective. I call it "funny vision."

Picture with me, if you would, a pair of those gigantic clown-like sunglasses. (I actually have several pairs that I choose from to use when I'm speaking on this topic. I always try to coordinate the right color of glasses with what I'm wearing. These glasses come in all colors, usually very bright colors. As if their size isn't enough to draw your attention!) Anyway, when life gets tough, sometimes it's best just to get those glasses, put them on, and go look at yourself in the mirror. It will change your perspective, I'm telling you!

Choosing to tap into "funny vision" can be a real life-saver for you. Often it's just the thing you'll need to survive some pretty bad stuff or some pretty tough days. My theory is if you have to laugh or cry, choose laughter as much as possible.

Barbara Johnson puts it this way, "Laughter is to life what shock absorbers are to automobiles. It won't take the potholes out of the road, but it sure makes the ride smoother."

God Can Walk On His Eyeballs

God says so, too, you know! Proverbs 17: 22 *"A cheerful heart is good medicine, but a crushed spirit dries up the bones."*

(New International Version)

The Message Bible puts it like this, *"A cheerful disposition is good for your health; gloom and doom leave you bone-tired."*

And in Ecclesiastes 3, God's Word says there *" is a time to weep and a time laugh."*

There's a story of a family whose father passed away suddenly and unexpectedly while on vacation several states away. They were horribly shocked and the grief of losing their beloved dad was nearly unbearable. While in mourning, they had to make the necessary funeral arrangements, which were complicated even more because they had to have the body flown home for the services.

The day of the funeral arrived and the family members were at the church when the funeral director came in with an unsettled expression on his face. The body had not arrived at the airport. The plane was delayed in another city due to bad weather. This dreadful news just added to their pain. The tears began to flow and each one whimpered quietly.

One of the children looked up and said to the rest of the family, "You know, we always said Dad would be late for his own funeral!"

It was just what they needed in that moment. Laughter through tears can be wonderful, healing medicine.

Personally, I love to laugh. Some of my favorite memories involve laughing so hard with a sister or friend that I – well let's just say that adult protective undergarments are in my future. I've had the pleasure of experiencing the "church giggles," the "you just had to be there laughs," and the "wheeze."

Cindy Foor

You know them, don't you?

The "church giggles" occur when you are supposed to be relatively serious, like when attending church or a meeting – someplace where breaking out into laughter would be the farthest thing from appropriate. But something happens.

This kind of laughter usually involves another person. No one else notices – it's just you and her at this point. Whatever it is that happened really isn't that funny, but as you look at one another, unable to speak, you smile and quietly laugh. Quickly, however, you look away. You have to because if you look at her again, you're going to laugh out loud.

In the corner of your eye, you notice she moved a little, so you look over. She's looking right at you! Oh, no! You're both giggling now, and neither of you knows why! Your attempt to quiet yourselves is futile and you begin to do the "shoulder shudder," which, if this is happening in church, has been known to shake the entire pew. This will definitely get the attention of those around you. Now you're a spectacle and you know it. Oh my stars! This is not good.

Tears begin to flow down your cheeks, your shoulders are shuddering uncontrollably now, and everyone around you is starting to laugh, too. The only way you can get out of this is to get up and get out of there. So you get up, still laughing, breathing highly irregularly, snorting, and crying. If the rest of the attendees didn't notice you before, they do now!

"Church giggles" often turn into the "you just had to be there laughs." "You just had to be there laughs" are the ones where you and someone else share a hilarious experience that only the two of you think is funny. No matter how hard you try to explain to others what happened, it's just not nearly as funny to them as it is to you and your friend. But the two of you can re-live the experience forever – and you do. Every time you're together, in fact, one of you brings it up and you laugh all over again, just as though it happened for the first time.

A word of caution - the people who don't get what's so funny will not enjoy it when you keep re-living it either. It wasn't funny to them the first time, and it will *never* be funny to them, because they just don't get it. They "just had to be there," remember? So since they weren't there the first time, try to be considerate of their feelings, ok? (Snicker.)

Now, the "wheeze" is my signature laugh! When something unexpectedly strikes me as "funny," I can't take any air in because I'm just wheezing it all out! When my lungs are completely devoid of all air, I can take a huge breath of new, fresh air. But that supply gets wheezed out just as the first one did.

This continues for many rounds of wheezing and sucking in air until I need the aforementioned protective undergarments or I pass out. I've been known to go for many rounds of wheezing. I've even gone several rounds, rested a bit, and started several more rounds. I'm a strong wheezing contender!

A "wheezer" sounds like that old cartoon character, Mutley. He was a dog who wheezed when he laughed. Are you old enough to remember him? Oh, forget it! "Google" him – he's still out there!

Laughter is such fun isn't it? And studies have been done that prove God's Word is accurate in this regard. (I just love when science catches up to God's truth!) These studies show that a good laugh can lower blood pressure, energize the body, boost the immune system, and relax muscles. When we laugh we become more intuitive, more compassionate, more attuned to those around us.

And here's a great one - one laugh burns 6 calories! Dr. William Fry of Stanford University says laughing heartily 100 times per day has the same beneficial effects as ten minutes on a rowing machine. Now *that's* my kind of exercise! I should be much thinner than I am, though.

Various studies also show that laughter goes hand in hand with creativity. People with a keen sense of humor have a more creative outlook to problem-solving than do somber individuals. Tests show that those who listened to a comedy album were able to withstand 20% more pain than those tested who were not exposed to humor. (Do you know what an "album" is? If not, "Google" that, too! You youngster!)

Have you seen the movie "Patch Adams" with actor Robin Williams? The movie is based on the true life happenings of Dr. "Patch" Adams, who knew these scientifically-proven facts - that laughter is healing for the body as well as for the spirit. He took this knowledge and shared his love through laughter and antics in hospitals with people who desperately needed this message of hope. Dr. Adams knew that medicine of laughter was highly effective.

Even the world knows that laughter is good medicine, but I wanted to research the Word of God further. I wanted to know what else God says about laughter. You might be surprised where I ended up. The book of Genesis! (Isn't that a knee-slapper? Not!)

In the book of Genesis, we learn about Abraham's response when he learned that he and Sarah were going to be parents to a son, Isaac. (The name, Isaac, actually means "laughter," by the way.) Look at Genesis 17:17 with me.

"Abraham fell face down; he laughed and said to himself, "Will a son be born to a man 100 years old? Will Sarah bear a child at the age of 90?"

(New International Version)

I read that and wondered, why did Abraham laugh? And why did God record in scripture the fact that Abraham laughed? What does

God Can Walk On His Eyeballs

God want us – living in this present age – to understand?

- Does He want us to understand that we should continue to have faith? Yes.

- That we can trust Him with our requests? Yes.

- That He has a plan for us? Yes.

- That His timetable is the *only* timetable that matters? Yes.

- That He knows what He's doing? Yes.

- That, with Him, all things are possible? Yes.

We can answer "absolutely yes" to each and every one of these questions. But what about the *laughter*?

"Abraham fell face down…"

His initial response was obviously worshipful reverence. Abraham knew this birth was something only the God of the Universe could do. He was humbling himself before God Almighty, in awe of His amazing power.

But while he was face down in reverent worship, he laughed. I don't believe he laughed at *what* God was doing. I believe he laughed at *how* God was going to do it.

God told Abraham that he was going to make him the "father of many nations." And Abraham just realized that God would fulfill that promise by making him a natural father at age 100, and his wife a natural mother at age 90.

Now, with no irreverence intended here, I think that's pretty funny. I think I'd react the same way! "Wow, God, you're wonderful. I'm humbled in your awesome presence. Only You can do this!"

"Now, what *exactly* did you say you were going to do? Would you please repeat that for me? I think I might have misunderstood You."

Did God ever do anything amazing in your life that was so creative, so far-fetched, so opposite of what you ever thought He'd do, that you just had to laugh? I'm sure you can think of some. Work like this is His specialty! It's one of His signature moves!

When Steve and I lived in Washington, DC, we'd travel up to Lancaster, Pennsylvania to visit my oldest sister, Debbie, and her family. We'd travel up Interstate 95, connect with 695 (the beltway around Baltimore), pick up Interstate 83 to York, and finally Route 30 to Lancaster. At that point in my life, my view of York, Pennsylvania was what I could see from Interstate 83 and a very small piece of Route 30. I intend no offense to York or anyone who lives there, but the view from those two highways isn't very pretty. It's all industrial buildings and vacant lots. Every single time we'd make this trip to visit Debbie, I'd actually say, "I will *never* live in York, Pennsylvania. Who would ever choose to live in this town?"

I'm certain that God in His heaven was looking down, shaking His head and chuckling at me. Because it was only a few years later that Steve took a job in York, Pennsylvania. If you recall, I wouldn't live in York at first. Initially, we lived in Lancaster for eleven months, and after that, Steve commuted from York to the Altoona area for two and half more years. (I'm strong-willed, in case I didn't tell you that already!)

But when both our children were entering school, Steve and I looked for a home in the York area. We found a great house, in a great neighborhood, in a great school district. And get this, I got down on my face and prayed to the God of the universe and asked Him to please, please, let us move our family to York, Pennsylvania! Then I laughed, and I laughed.

I'm telling you, this God of ours works in ways we cannot understand. We must stop trying to dictate or guess or manipulate His answers to our prayers or His plans for our lives. You simply cannot put this God neatly in a box. He's way too big for that! He's so much more creative than that! His ways are not our ways! His thoughts are so much higher than our thoughts!

The next time God shows you something big, something powerful, something so far-fetched about Himself, may I suggest you respond just as Abraham did? Put yourself face down in humble, reverent worship that you have the privilege of knowing this great, mighty, powerful God. Bow to His authority. Submit to His divine plan.

Then put on those big clown sunglasses and laugh! Laugh with joy about how creative He is. Laugh with delight about how wonderful He is. Laugh about how intimately, intricately involved in the lives of His children He is.

That's exactly what I plan to do after I finish writing the last word of this book. What He'll do with it, I don't know. But how He thought of *me* to write it – the strong-willed, stubborn, rebellious child – now that's a hoot!

He is so amazing!

Chapter 6
"I Can Love Other Like Jesus Does"

I love people. I really do. They fascinate me and intrigue me. They frustrate me and make me crazy, too. I'm sure you know what I'm talking about.

I always knew that people were important to God. I mean, look at the story of how He created man and woman, and you'll see that people are clearly His priority. God's Word says each of us are "fearfully and wonderfully made." (Some of us are more fearful than others!)

But when the disciples asked Jesus if He would sum up all of the commandments and explain to them which one is the *most* important, Jesus responded with these words:

"Love the Lord your God with all your heart and with all your soul and with all your mind. This is the first and greatest com-

mandment. And the second is like it: Love your neighbor as yourself."

(Matthew 22:37-39 New International Version)

The answer Jesus gave was clear to say that God is first, people are next. Both are extremely important.

But if you're like me, even if you like people in general, there are always those people who come into your life who, quite frankly, are just not that lovable. Do you have any of those? (Perhaps *you* are one of them for someone else! I'm quite sure I am!) And God doesn't say "put up with them," or "ignore them and eventually they'll go away." No, no. God says "love your neighbor as yourself."

1 Corinthians 13 gives a beautiful description of what God's love looks like. It's a well-known passage, often recited at weddings.

"If I speak in the tongues of men and of angels, but have not love, I am only a resounding gong or a clanging cymbal. If I have the gift of prophecy and can fathom all mysteries and all knowledge, and if I have a faith that can move mountains, but have not love, I am nothing. If I give all I possess to the poor and surrender my body to the flames, but have not love, I gain nothing."

"Love is patient, love is kind. It does not envy, it does not boast, it is not proud. It is not rude, it is not self-seeking, it is not easily angered, it keeps no record of wrongs. Love does not delight in evil but rejoices with the truth. It always protects, always trusts, always hopes, always perseveres."

"Love never fails. But where there are prophecies, they will cease; where there are tongues, they will be stilled; where there is knowledge, it will pass away. For we know in part and we prophesy in part, but when perfection comes, the imperfect disappears.

God Can Walk On His Eyeballs

When I was a child, I talked like a child, I thought like a child, I reasoned like a child. When I became a man, I put childish ways behind me. Now we see but a poor reflection as in a mirror; then we shall see face to face. Now I know in part; then I shall know fully, even as I am fully known."

"And now these three remain: faith, hope and love. But the greatest of these is love."

(New International Version)

The first three verses of this passage are so powerful. Basically, regardless of what I do, regardless of my gifts, abilities, knowledge, and faith, if I don't live my life with love as my motivation, the result is meaningless. I am only making noise. I am nothing. I am accomplishing nothing.

Love is the key to everything about our God. It's the very reason He created us – to have a relationship with Him. And when we messed that up, it was His love that provided the way back to a relationship with Him, through Jesus. And it His love that held Jesus on the cross, it wasn't the nails. He was God, after all. He could have chosen to not go down the road to Golgotha; to avoid the crucifixion; to allow us to remain separated from God. But He didn't, because of His love, His amazing love.

The original text of this passage in scripture uses the word "agape" for "love." "Agape" is a divine capacity to love. Only God is capable of agape love. Yet the very same word – "agape" – is used in the passage in Matthew 22 when we are instructed to love God and love our neighbors.

I wrestled with this one, especially in view of some "difficult" people who enter my life. How was I supposed to love others with "agape" love when only God is capable of loving that way? I mean, look at what God's love looks like!

41

God's love is patient, kind, it doesn't envy, it's not boastful, not proud. It is not rude, it is not self-seeking, it is not easily angered, it does not keep a record of wrongs. That's just the partial list! I failed on the first quality of patience! The thing God taught me about love is this. Because He loves me this way, and because I received Christ as my Savior, Christ now lives in me. Because Christ lives in me, I am capable of loving others just like God does when I allow Him to love others through me. Does that make sense?

Well, then. Easy enough, right? Not for me, it isn't! It's not easy because it involves that "s" word again – surrender. In order for me to be obedient to God's Word and love others, I must surrender to God's way of loving others and let Him love them through me. Oh, sometimes don't you wish you could've been there when Jesus was talking so you could ask some questions just as the disciples did? When He answered their question about the greatest commandment, I just know my next question would've been, "But exactly *how* are we supposed to do that? We don't even like everyone!"

Allow me to share with you how God has personally answered this question in my life. He keeps sending people to me. They won't go away. I tell you, I know right away when God is proving to me that I really can love others like He does. Usually, they irritate me from the start! (Now at this point, if you're reading this and you know me, you're most likely worried that *you* are one of those people. Please let me assure you – you might be! But hey! The good news is that I love you, I really do love you! But this particular story is *not* about you, ok?)

Many years ago, God crossed my path with a woman who is probably the most oppositely natured woman from me. She's just so different from me – our taste in clothing, décor, books, movies, food, conversation, everything - was different. We really agreed on very little. And, quite honestly, she bugged me. She got on my nerves. (I am sure that she felt the same way about me!)

So I decided that I would deal with her only when I had to, only when absolutely necessary, and I would be polite, but brief in my dealings. But God had other plans. Through a series of circumstances, God placed this woman in my life with almost daily contact. I thought I'd go out of my mind. Then it dawned on me.

"You're behind this, aren't You, God? I know how you work. This is another of Your signature moves!"

I told Him, "Ok, then. If she won't go away, You're just going to have to love her through me!" Deep down, I knew that's exactly what He was after in my heart. So I surrendered to Him and prayed that He would show me how to be patient, kind, not irritable, etc. And I prayed for her.

Through one instance after another, God was faithful to His Word and my prayers. Let me tell you, I had to pray a lot about her. But today, I can honestly say, from the depths of my heart, that I genuinely "agape" love this woman. We've been friends for years despite our immense differences. She still makes me crazy sometimes, and I still make her crazy sometimes, but we love each other.

So I remember thinking, "Cool! I'm done now. God, you can check that one off your list of things to teach me. I get it. I passed the test. Yea, me!" But He had other plans. Along came the next person. You see, they'll keep coming, these people. They won't go away either.

If I already learned this lesson about loving people like God does, why would God keep sending these people to me? Because it's not about them – it's about me. God wants to work on my heart. I learned the basic message, the main idea of what He's teaching me, but I haven't perfected it yet. He has more refining to do.

I used to think that I was pretty wonderful – loving "unlovable" people, just like Jesus tells us to. I thought, "Well, someone needs to do it. I guess God will use me." As though God thought, "I'll send them to Cindy. She'll do it. She'll love anybody." (Kind of like Mikey and the cereal?)

But then I realized, God was really thinking, "I'll send them to Cindy because she still hasn't gotten it down right. She needs to learn more about loving people My way. She's learning with each one I send her about how wide and long and high and deep My love is for people. As she loves others My way, she'll realize more and more how much I love her."

Who is God laying on your heart right now? You know who they are. They're most likely the biggest frustrations of your day or week. They won't go away, will they? God has divine purpose for them and has uniquely devised a way to cross your path with theirs.

It's not so you can do something wonderful for them. It's so He can do something wonderful for *you*! Allow Him to love *through* you. You might just find your best friend. But you'll definitely have a better grasp of His wide, long, high, and deep love for you.

Oh, the love of God is truly amazing, isn't it?

"And I pray that you, being rooted and established in love, may have power, together with all the saints, to grasp how wide and long and high and deep is the love of Christ, and to know this love that surpasses knowledge – that you may be filled to the measure of all the fullness of God."

(Ephesians 3:17b-19 New International Version)

Chapter 7
"Spiritual Battles Are Real"

The life lesson God taught me in this chapter was one of the biggest eye-openers I've ever had in my Christian walk to date.

I knew there was a "devil," and I knew his name was "Satan," or "Lucifer." But I never really knew much more than that. And as a child of God, I needed to know much more than that. What I learned about spiritual battles leads right into my next chapter about spiritual freedom, because that's what the battles are all about – true freedom.

The enemy doesn't want God's children to be free, spiritually. He knows he cannot touch our salvation – if you've received Jesus Christ as your personal Savior, you're already considered by God as "seated in the heavenly realms with Christ." (See Chapter 4,

"Who I Am in Christ is My True Identity.") As far as God is concerned, you are already a "citizen of heaven." So Satan cannot do anything to jeopardize that.

Romans 8:38-39 puts it this way. *"For I am convinced that neither death nor life, neither angels nor demons, neither the present nor the future, nor any powers, neither height nor depth, nor anything else in all creation, will be able to separate us from the love of God that is in Christ Jesus our Lord."*

(New International Version)

But despite his inability to steal your gift of eternal life, Satan has a very detailed strategy to steal your joy, your peace, your contentment, your impact for Christ in this world. His plan is to render Christians useless for the kingdom of Christ.

Like it or not, if you are a child of God, you are at war! Allow me to share with you what God taught me about spiritual battles. I call it the "A-B-C's of the Battle."

A – Our Adversary

Honestly, I don't like to talk about our enemy. But unless we have an understanding of who he is and how he works, we won't be properly equipped for battle. And if we aren't well equipped, how will we be victorious? So not to puff him up or to glorify him in any way, let's learn what God teaches us about our adversary.

Children of God have an enemy who is ruthless and cunning. He has a detailed strategy; he engages you through lies; he seduces you with temptation; he has a counter plan against God's will for your life; he aims at anything that resembles Jesus Christ, whom he hates.

In John 10:10, Jesus teaches that Satan – called here the "thief" - came to *"steal, kill and destroy."*

2 Corinthians 11:14-15 explains that *"Satan himself masquerades as an angel of light,"* and *"his servants masquerade as servants of righteousness."*

In John 8:44 Jesus tells us that *"....he (Satan) was a liar from the beginning, not holding to the truth, for there is no truth in him. When he lies, he speaks his native language, for he is a liar and the father of lies."*

(New International Version)

And that's exactly how he works – he lies! You've heard them, I'm sure.

- "You're not smart enough to do that."

- "Who do you think you are? Nobody wants to hear what you have to say."

- "You'll just fail, as you always do. Why even bother trying?"

- "You're not worth anything."

- "God will never really forgive you. Your past is too horrific!"

- "One more piece of cake won't hurt."

- "You're not good enough."

- "You don't need to go to church. That's where the hypocrites are."

- "You're a horrible mother."

- "You're a weak Christian. You're nothing like Him."

- "There is no way out. It's hopeless."

- "No one will ever understand."

- "No one will miss you if you're gone."

Oh, yes, our adversary is really good at lying. He knows how to hit right where it hurts. How does he do that? It's important that you realize that Satan cannot read your mind. He does not have the power to read or know your thoughts. But Satan can *interject* thoughts, which are almost always lies. How does he know which lies will hurt the most? Which lies will do the most damage?

He knows because he studies you. He studies your behavior patterns. He watches how you react to life's curve balls. He figures out your weaknesses, and he plans his attack accordingly. Satan has one goal – to deceive and control your mind.

- If you tend to be insecure, guess where he plans his attack?

- If you struggle with food addictions, that's when chocolate cake or mashed potatoes with lots of butter are always right there in front of you.

- Perhaps your battle is addiction to other substances – alcohol, tobacco, drugs. They're available everywhere you look, aren't they?

- If you worry about everything, he'll delight in watching you attempt to handle issue after issue, problem after problem. He loves to watch you get anxious and fret over things.

- If you struggle with lust, people who are attractive to you will inevitably cross your path. Even your dream life will be affected.

- If spending too much money is your problem, sale after sale will come to your attention – right in your mailbox. (And did you know that Satan knows how to use email?)

- If your battle is forgiving someone, he'll constantly remind you of the one who hurt you.

- If you are obsessed with perfection – trying to do everything you're "supposed to do" - the perfect home, the perfect wife, the perfect children, the perfect Christian, the perfect neighbor, the perfect woman - he'll trip you up every time.

After studying you, he knows where you're most susceptible, where your "jugular" is located. Your vulnerability is his playground, and he will use your vulnerability against you as much as he possibly can.

Where does all of this activity, this lying, take place? Where is this battle fought?

B - The Battle

2 Corinthians 11:3 says *"But I am afraid that just as Eve was deceived by the serpent's cunning, your minds may somehow be led astray from your sincere and pure devotion to Christ."*

(New International Version)

Eve was deceived by lies from the serpent adversary. Where did he attack her? Her mind. The mind – your mind, my mind - is the location of the battlefield. Kind of scary, huh? Hang in there. There's a plan! Let's press on through this passage.

We know the location, what about the battle itself? How is it fought? 2 Corinthians 10 teaches so much about this.

"For though we live in the world, we do not wage war as the world does. The weapons we fight with are not the weapons of the world. On the contrary, they have divine power to demolish

strongholds. We demolish arguments and every pretension that sets itself up against the knowledge of God, and we take captive every thought to make it obedient to Christ."

(2 Corinthians 10:3-5 New International Version)

Three things about the battle are evident in verses 3 and 4 of this passage:

1. We do not wage war as the world does.

2. Our weapons are not weapons of this world.

3. Our weapons have divine power to demolish strongholds.

In a minute, we'll talk about our weapons, but first, what exactly is a "stronghold?" Paul defines a stronghold in verse 5 as *"any argument or pretension that sets itself up against the knowledge of God."* A pretension is anything that is pretending to be bigger or more powerful than God.

A stronghold is exactly what it implies – it's something that has a "strong hold" on your mind – a grip on your thought life. A stronghold is anything that captures your focus - demands a lot of your thinking time - often your brain becomes obsessed with the thoughts. A stronghold is anything that sets itself in a place higher than God Almighty, who should be your number one focus; number one of all your thoughts. (Remember the most important commandment?)

And as we've already discussed, this is exactly what our adversary has outlined in his strategy against us! It's his goal to capture our minds – using lies to get our focus off of God - and lead us into bondage (captivity) rendering us useless for Christ.

That's his goal, but according to this passage, what should *our* goal be?

Verse 5 says *"We demolish arguments and every pretension that sets itself up against the knowledge of God, and we take captive every thought to make it obedient to Christ."*

Our goal is twofold:

1. To demolish strongholds, and

2. To take our thoughts captive to Christ.

The obvious next question is "How are strongholds demolished?"

First, we must know what weapons of warfare are available to us. This passage teaches that they are not weapons of this world and they have divine power. And in Ephesians 6:10-18, the whole armor of God is described. Let's quickly look at this important passage before we answer this question.

"Finally, be strong in the Lord and in His mighty power. Put on the full armor of God so that you can take your stand against the devil's schemes. For our struggle is not against flesh and blood, but against the rulers, against the authorities, against the powers of this dark world and against the spiritual forces of evil in the heavenly realms."

"Therefore, put on the full armor of God, so that when the day of evil comes, you may be able to stand your ground, and after you have done everything, to stand."

"Stand firm then, with the belt of truth buckled around your waist, with the breastplate of righteousness in place, and with your feet fitted with the readiness that comes from the gospel of peace."

"In addition to all this, take up the shield of faith, with which you can extinguish all the flaming arrows of the evil one."

"Take the helmet of salvation and the sword of the Spirit, which is the Word of God."

Cindy Foor

"And pray in the Spirit on all occasions with all kinds of prayer and requests. With this in mind, be alert and always keep on praying for all the saints."

(New International Version)

Of all of the armor that God provides, only one is a weapon of offense – all of the others are defensive pieces of armor – to protect us. The helmet, the belt, the breastplate, the shoes, etc. The only offensive weapon is the "sword of the Spirit, which is the Word of God."

But the previous passage we looked at 2 Corinthians 10: 3 tells us that we have *weapons*, plural. We have the sword of the Spirit – the Word of God – but what other weapon do we have?

Look again at Ephesians 6, verse 18. *"And pray in the Spirit on all occasions."* Prayer is our other major weapon of offense. Without prayer, we are not in communication with the Commander-in-chief! Our main supply chain is highly endangered. Our lifeline is cut off.

These two weapons – the sword of the truth (the Word of God) and prayer are crucial to our victory in spiritual battles.

2 Corinthians 10:4 says that our weapons have *"divine power to demolish strongholds."* Cool! The Greek word used here is the adjective form of "dynamai," which means "to be able, with the achieving power of God applied." Our English word "dynamite" is derived from this Greek word. What is God saying here?

He's saying that our weapons of divine power are like dynamite! And dynamite will demolish strongholds! Strongholds cannot be swept from our minds or ignored and they'll go away. They must be demolished, and they can only be demolished with divine power. God's power. His weapons of the Word of truth and prayer.

(Did you ever notice how many times we Christians are told to study God's Word and to pray? There's a reason, my dear friends! There's a really good reason!)

C – Our Counter Plan

Now, what's our game plan? What's our strategy? What's our counter plan against our adversary?

Our goal is to take our thoughts captive and make them obedient to Christ, according to verse 5 of 2 Corinthians 10. I call this the "Take and Make" strategy, and really, it's pretty clear cut.

We are to take captive the thoughts that are lies – reject them – and replace them with thoughts of truth. Where do we find truth? The Word of God - one of our most important weapons of offense.

For example, the enemy is relentless to attack me when I'm preparing to speak or even as I was writing this book. He always says things to me like, "Who do you think you are? You're not Beth Moore! You're just Cindy Foor. You don't have a degree. You're not capable of writing a book. You'll embarrass yourself. You will fail."

(Now, don't go feeling sorry for me. I've learned to recognize the lies of my enemy and I know how to battle him now.) Here's what I have to do when he whispers his garbage to me. I have to take the lies captive and replace it with truth. To him, I say "I am not a failure – I am a child of God. It is God Almighty who makes me adequate to do this work. He has equipped me with everything good for doing His will."

And where did I get this truth? Right out of the Word of God!

- I am a child of God – John 1:12

- He makes me adequate – 2 Corinthians 3:5-6

- He equips me with everything good for doing His will – Hebrews 13:21

And you better believe I prayed! I have a team of faithful prayer warriors just waiting for me to call with my requests. I am so thankful for them!

The "A-B-C's of the Battle:"

- Know your ADVERSARY – the enemy – be aware of his tactics and his strategy.

- Understand the BATTLE is in your mind – the battle is for control of your mind. You don't have to give any ground over to the enemy.

- Your COUNTERPLAN is "Take and Make" – reclaim your thoughts for Christ. You have weapons of divine power – dynamite – and with them, you can demolish strongholds.

One final thought for you about spiritual warfare. You must remember this Word of truth and hide it in your heart, ok?

1 John 4:4 says, ***"You, dear children, are from God and have overcome them,*** (Paul is writing here about overcoming evil spirits) ***because the One who is in you is greater than the one who is in the world."***

(New International Version)

If you received Jesus Christ as your Savior, God calls you His "child." When you became a child of God, the spirit of God came to live in you. While your strength and your power are useless in these battles, please remember that He who lives in you is greater than he who lives in the world.

This great God is amazing!

Chapter 8
"I Must Live My Freedom in Christ"

As I began to wrap my brain around the things I was learning about spiritual warfare, and as I was learning how to biblically respond to spiritual attacks, I realized that there was yet another facet to this whole subject I had somehow missed all these years. I wondered, "Why was the enemy attacking me? What did he want from me? What has he already taken from me?"

It took time and prayer, but eventually I discovered that while Satan was deceiving me for a very long time, I had allowed him to have some ground that didn't belong to him. I was finally catching up to all those years of believing his lies, and there were some areas of bondage I had to deal with. For such a long time, I never even realized I was in captivity!

For the first time in my life, I understood what my freedom was all about. It was *my* freedom, given to me by Jesus Christ, and I had to learn how to live it. Now that I realized I had been held captive, all I wanted was my freedom! And I knew where to turn next.

In the book of Galatians, Paul is writing to believers to make sure they understand their salvation is solely dependent upon God's grace, not on works. Our freedom is in Christ alone and what He did for us on the cross – we can do nothing to earn it.

Galatians 5:1(a) *"It is for freedom that Christ has set us free."*

(New International Version)

And this particular verse makes that very clear. Christ died to set us free from the yoke of the Law. If you received Christ as your Savior, His death and subsequent resurrection has qualified you to be placed under the Law of grace and you are no longer under condemnation of the Law. You are free!

The second part of this verse Galatians 5:1(b) says *"Stand firm, then, and do not let yourselves be burdened again by a yoke of slavery."*

See the "stand firm" there? The word used here is the same word Paul used in Ephesians 6 where we are told to stand, wearing the full protection of God's armor. It means to be steadfast, immovable in our knowledge of who we are "in Christ."

"...and do not let yourselves be burdened again..." The language used here for "burden" means to allow yourself to be in opposition, to be hostile toward something.

"...by a yoke of slavery..." To be under an oppressed condition. To be in bondage.

To paraphrase this verse, *"Stand firm in who you are in Christ, and do not let yourselves be in opposition again with any bondage or sin."*

To put the verse all together, Galatians 5:1 says *"It is for freedom that Christ has set us free. Stand firm, then, and do not let yourselves be burdened again by a yoke of slavery."*

(New International Version)

Two questions immediately came to mind as I studied this wonderful verse:

1. What is it that enslaves me?

2. How can I get free – and stay free - from it?

Let's look at each of these questions, one at a time…

What is it that enslaves me? My first thought was, well that verse says that Christ has set me free, so how can I be enslaved? But then I remembered that the book of Galatians is written to believers who have already received Christ as their personal Savior. Believers must be susceptible to bondage and enslavement, because God cautions us here against allowing it.

So what is bondage? Bondage is anything that keeps you from your freedom:

- IT controls *you!*

- IT controls your *thoughts.*

- IT controls your *focus.*

- IT controls your *time.*

- IT controls your *energy.*

These areas are meant for God – alone. You were created and called to love the Lord your God with all your heart, with all your soul, with all your mind, and with all your strength. Any substitutes will never make the grade. Our Savior did, indeed, save us from eternal separation from God, but He also keeps on saving us by empowering us to remain free!

But let's get this part straight. If you do not know Jesus Christ as your personal Savior – if you have never made the choice to receive his gift of salvation – if your knowledge of Him has not yet made the trip from your head to your heart – if you attend church regularly, pray before meals, attend Bible study religiously – but you don't have a *relationship* with Him – if you believe in Him, but never *received* Him and his free gift – you are <u>not</u> free.

You cannot be free without Him! This must be your first step! If, with these words, I am describing you – if these words ring all too familiarly with you, you must make a decision regarding Jesus. What will you do with Him? He's offering you eternal life, and eternity begins the moment you receive Him. There's no cost for this gift. There's nothing you can do to earn it. He offers it just because He loves you. There is no decision more important than this in your entire life. Not receiving Him is choosing to reject Him, by the way. But He's a polite God. He won't push His way into your life. He's done all of the work. You just have to accept it, or reject it. I urge you to make your decision to receive Him. You have everything to gain!

But some of you have already made that decision, and you do have a relationship with Him. Yet you can't quite figure out how to live – daily live - in the freedom that Jesus provides. You struggle. Your enemy wrestles with you. And many of you battle secretly with things like:

- Depression

- Alcoholism

- Drugs

- Food addictions

- Perhaps exercise has become your "god."

- Some of you are shop-aholics. You keep spending money unnecessarily, justifying your purchases with "but it was such a great sale price!"

- Some of you live in the fantasy world of romance novels – even those written by Christian authors can be dangerous for some.

- Some have crossed the line into pornography.

- Perhaps your battle is self-worth. You don't feel worthy of anything good from God.

- Your prison is guilt from your past sin.

- Or maybe you just cannot bring yourself to forgive that one person. You forgave everyone else, but you just have to hang onto that one a little longer. When you feel a little better about it you'll forgive.

- Many of you attempt to live up to others' expectations of you. If you don't measure up, you're less of a person or less of a Christian.

- Is fear your stronghold? Fear of the future? Fear of failure? Fear of success?

- Some of you are contemplating adultery.

- Some of you have already made contact with another man.

- Some of you have already committed adultery.

- Perhaps you've struggled all your life with thoughts of homosexuality.

- Maybe you've experienced it.

- Some of you live in a world of extreme loneliness. You put on a happy face and do all the right things, but deep down inside, your heart is breaking and you have little faith that God sees you suffering.

- Maybe discouragement is your daily comrade.

- Are you an expert on alluding peace, and joy, and contentment? More wrapped up in the circumstances of your life than on who your God is?

Beth Moore, in her study entitled "Breaking Free" wrote these words:

"How would I have known that I was lost had You not searched and found me? How would I have known that I was blind had You not made me see? How would I have known my bleeding 'til You bound your love around me? How would I have groaned my slavery until You set me free?"

She said, "I had no idea I was in captivity until God began to set me free."

There are so many of us like her. We, who are believers in Christ struggle every day, don't we? If Christ has set us free, why do we struggle?

For me, a key was the phrase "do not let yourselves." Oh my stars! That was powerful to me. Do you ever read a verse of scripture and it just hits you right between your eyes? That one little phrase did that to me. Jesus paid such a dear price to set me free from bondage, yet I, as a believer, am cautioned to not *let myself* become burdened by a yoke of slavery again. Could it be that I *allow* myself to be enslaved? Absolutely!

As a believer in Christ, if I am - if you are - living in bondage, **it is voluntary.** Voluntary. We have *"let ourselves become burdened by the yoke of slavery."* We let it happen.

My dear friends, it is imperative that you understand that which enslaves you – that to which you are susceptible – the area(s) of your life with which you struggle. Not because I like to talk about your sinfulness or my sinfulness! But because if you understand your yoke of slavery, you can know where your enemy is planning his attack, and you must begin to allow the power of Christ to set you free!

What enslaves you? I believe deep down, you know what it is. God certainly knows what it is, and your enemy knows what it is. Please, be honest with yourself. I believe it's time that we believers stop justifying our sin, our bondage. It's time to stop acting like everything's just fine – like we've got it all together – like none of us struggles with sin. It's time to stop glossing over it. It's time to stop deceiving ourselves.

I've been told by many women that they honestly believe they are the only ones who don't have it all together. They really do believe that they are the only ones who struggle with sin. Or they believe their sin is greater than everyone else's sin – that they're much bigger sinners than others. It always makes me wonder how pretentious are we Christians that others think we've got it all together?

My response is always the same to these women. "Please don't believe for one minute that you have cornered the market on sin. We all sin. None of us has it all together. No, not one!" Identify that which enslaves you and get on to the next step!

The 2nd question: How can I get free – and stay free - from that which enslaves me?

Look at Galatians 5, beginning with verse 16….

"So, I say live by the Spirit, and you will not gratify the desires of the sinful nature. For the sinful nature desires what is contrary to the Spirit, and the Spirit what is contrary to the sinful nature. They are in conflict with each other, so that you do not do what you want. But, if you are led by the Spirit, you are not under law."

Skip to verses 24 & 25....

"Those who belong to Christ Jesus have crucified the sinful nature with its passions and desires. Since we live by the Spirit, let us keep in step with the Spirit."

This is so important to your victory, to gaining your freedom. Look at verse 16 where it says *"live by the Spirit."* The word used here is in the present tense, meaning to "go on living" in the Spirit. It's a daily practice. Continuing to live by the Spirit, not by your flesh or its desires. And in verse 18, if you are *"led by the Spirit,"* it means you listen to Him. You live daily, allowing the Holy Spirit of God to lead you. It's a surrender and submission to His leading.

Your freedom - and your ability to stay free - is in the power of the Holy Spirit. You just aren't powerful enough! Determining to become free from bondage, to attempt to free yourself, to tap into your own will power, will *not* work! This does not mean that we will not struggle with sin, but it does mean that we can have victory in the struggle through the power of the Holy Spirit and the level with which we live by Him and walk with Him.

Verses 22-23 of Galatians 5 explain what living by the Spirit looks like. *"But the fruit of the Spirit is love, joy, peace, patience, kindness, goodness, gentleness, and self-control. Against such things there is no law."*

(New International Version)

"There is no law." In other words, there is freedom in these things! Love, joy, peace, patience, kindness, goodness, gentleness

and self-control are available to you through the Holy Spirit who lives in you, if you are "in Christ."

Christian character is produced by the Holy Spirit, not by us trying to live by law. It is the indwelling Holy Spirit who produces Christ-like characteristics in us. If any of these characteristics listed touch a nerve with you, by the way, (love, joy, peace, patience, kindness, goodness, gentleness, self-control), most likely you are in some type of bondage in this area.

For example, self-control is the one that always jumps out of that list for me. And yes, self-control is the area I struggle with the most - my eating, my spending, balancing my time, my love of purses! (There, I said it!)

Perhaps patience jumps off the page for you. Or gentleness. Whatever jumps out at you, is most likely an area of susceptibility to sin in your life. When nerves are touched or words jump off pages of scripture, that's one of the ways the Holy Spirit works to convict you of sin. It's one of His signature moves. Pay attention to Him! It's for your own good that you deal with it!

And finally, in verse 25 we read *"Since we live by Spirit, let us keep in step with the Spirit."* Keeping in step with the Spirit means to walk in line with the Spirit, to stay with Him, to follow Him.

So according to these verses, how do I get free – and stay free – from that which enslaves me?

Please note Three Keys:

1. Verse 16 – Live by the Spirit – not by flesh

2. Verse 18 – Led by the Spirit – submit to His leadership, follow Him

3. Verse 25 – Keep in step with the Spirit – walk in alignment with Him – every day

Cindy Foor

Each of these keys require that we know the Spirit of God. We know His heart, we hear His voice, we are in His Word, and we live by His will.

There is no better way to live by Him, to be led by Him, or to keep in step with Him than to spend time with Him – in prayer and in His Word. No better way to know His heart, His voice, His will than to commune with Him. His communication to you is His Word. Your communication to Him is prayer. Sound like a familiar coupling? I'm telling you, they're essential to your freedom!

My dear brothers and sisters in Christ, living your freedom is God's plan for you. It's His heart's desire. It's the very reason He laid down His life for you. He wants His children to live every day in the freedom He provides – the freedom for which He died. Oh, how it must grieve Him to watch us voluntarily walk back into prison cells and close the doors to our freedom. Forgive us, Jesus. May we not take for granted or minimize the magnitude of your gift of grace!

The doors have all been unlocked, my friends, and Jesus is the key holder – the keys of heaven and hell – of life and of death - are in the hands of your King! The One who holds the keys, has complete control over the domain, and He has opened the doors to your freedom.

Do you want to be free? Do you really want to be free?

Then lift up your hands and surrender those chains of bondage to the One who holds the keys!

Live by the Spirit, be led by the Spirit, and stay in step with the Spirit. It was for your freedom that Christ has set you free!

Amazing love!

Chapter 9

"God Wants an Intimate Relationship With Me"

I have chosen a passage of scripture that I call my own. These verses mirror my life so well. It's as though the Apostle Paul wrote them for me. Some people call this kind of discovery their "life verses." If you don't have any, look for one and claim it as your own. Hide it in your heart. May I share mine with you?

(I just love typing the words of these verses out again, and as I do so, I speak them aloud. The Word of God is infiltrating my heart through my eyes (both in my Bible and on my computer screen), through my lips as I read aloud, and through my ears as I hear what I'm repeating. I just love it!)

"But whatever was to my profit I now consider loss for the sake of Christ. What is more, I consider everything a loss compared to the surpassing greatness of knowing Christ Jesus, my Lord, for

whose sake I have lost all things. I consider them rubbish, that I may gain Christ and be found in Him, not having a righteousness of my own that comes from the law, but that which is through faith in Christ – the righteousness that comes from God and is by faith. I want to know Christ and the power of His resurrection and the fellowship of sharing in His sufferings, becoming like Him in His death, and so, somehow to attain to the resurrection from the dead."

(Philippians 3:7-11 New International Version)

Of all the things I have accomplished, of all my talents and abilities, of all my successes, of all I have acquired, of all the experiences of my life, there is *nothing* that can compare to the surpassing greatness of knowing Christ Jesus, my Lord.

I remember the first time I read that passage and realized it expressed exactly what I was feeling about Jesus. Knowing Him, not just knowing *about* Him, was the most wonderful thing that ever happened to me. And just as the verse in Psalm 34 says, ***"Taste and see that the Lord is good,"*** once I "tasted" Him – and realized how good He is - I wanted more. So I dug into the Word of God again to see what He had to say about our relationship. I wanted to look at it from His point of view. Here's what He taught me.

In Psalm 139 I read that I was fearfully and wonderfully made, and that God knit me together in my mother's womb. (I just love that word picture! My scary mind sees God sitting there with these big old knitting needles, "Knit one, pearl two. Knit one, pearl two. Now, for Cindy, a "special" stitch. I'll call it "orneriness!")

In Jeremiah 24:7 God says, ***"I will give them a heart to know me, that I am the Lord. They will be my people, and I will be their God, for they will return to me with all their heart."***

And in Jeremiah 29:13 He says, ***"You will seek me and find me when you seek me with all your heart."***

God Can Walk On His Eyeballs

And in Acts 17:27 Paul writes, *"God did this so that men would seek Him and perhaps reach out for Him and find Him, though He is not far from us."*

(New International Version)

So if God created me with a heart to know Him, with a heart to seek Him and reach out for Him, that must mean that He really wants a relationship with me!

I knew I strongly desired a deeper relationship with Him, but I never thought for a minute that *He* strongly desired a deeper relationship with *me*. What could *I* possibly offer *Him* in this relationship? What would the God of the universe want with *me*?

Then I read Jeremiah 31:3. *"The LORD appeared to us in the past, saying: 'I have loved you with an everlasting love; I have drawn you with loving-kindness.'"*

(New International Version)

This verse says that God has always loved me and has drawn me to Himself with loving-kindness. Wow! I mean, I knew that "Jesus Loves Me," and He died on the cross out of that love for me. But I never really thought about His desire to have a deeper, more intimate relationship with me. It was so humbling!

He actually created me to have a deep need for an intimate relationship with Him! All of a sudden it became so clear. The deepest desires of my heart – the things I have searched for all my life - are grounded in the very need God created me to have. God created this need in me so I would seek Him and find Him!

Oh, the years I wasted looking for Him in all the wrong places! My deep needs for intimacy, for trust, for affirmation, and for unconditional love could only be met in Him.

I can't tell you how many women I encounter who don't understand this truth. Like I did, they search and they search and they search. And it's not surprising, is it? This deep need is wired into how we are made, so we *will* search for the right thing to fill it because it's an emptiness we all have.

And our level of satisfaction in life depends on what we pour into this empty space in our souls. If we attempt to fill our souls with anything other than God Himself, we will never be satisfied. But, if we fill it with Him, we *will be* satisfied, because that's how we were created. He's the perfect match! Some call it the "God-shaped vacuum." A space that only God can fill.

- How's the satisfaction level of your soul right now?

- Do you have a deep yearning that never seems to be satisfied?

- Is your heart hungry?

- Is your soul thirsty?

That food you're trying to comfort yourself with won't work. The man you're contemplating having an affair with won't meet your needs. The alcohol or drug only deadens the mind for a little while. Your work might make you feel more accomplished and you might enjoy a successful career, but the accolades you receive won't fulfill you for long.

Please get this, my dear friends. **Only God can satisfy your soul.** If you're hungry or thirsty, it's your God calling you. He created you to seek Him. He wants you to find Him. He offers the most amazing relationship you'll ever have. Respond to Him and allow Him to satisfy your hunger and your thirst. Aren't you tired of searching?

"If anyone is thirsty, let him come to me and drink. Whoever believes in me, as the scripture has said, streams of living water will flow from within him."

(Jesus Christ – in John 7:37-38 New International Version)

Chapter 10
"Running the Race is Worth It"

I don't know how I ever survived the first 30 years of my life without consuming the Word of God. I say "consuming" because I had read it before – even memorized it. But I was 30 years old before I really began to consume it. The nourishment of His Word is life-sustaining. Without it, I would starve. It's why I love it so much. I must have it in order to live.

In a variety of passages of scripture the life of the Christian believer is compared to a race. There's one passage in particular that God used to teach me so much about living my life His way. It's found in Hebrews 12, verses 1-3.

"Therefore, since we are surrounded by such a great cloud of witnesses, let us throw off everything that hinders and the sin that so easily entangles, and let us run with perseverance the

race marked out for us. Let us fix our eyes on Jesus, the author and perfecter of our faith, who for the joy set before Him endured the cross, scorning its shame, and sat down at the right hand of the throne of God. Consider Him who endured such opposition from sinful men, so that you will not grow weary and lose heart."

(New International Version)

Are you a runner? I am not. I never was. I honestly don't get what all the hub-bub is about. Most runners I know get up ridiculously early to "do the run" and will run in all sorts of weather. To them, I guess, it's like my morning coffee. Gotta have it!

Me? I'd rather swim. Now that's a sport I can get into! You can work out without sweating. (I hate to sweat!) And because of the water pressure against your body, your body doesn't even know it's working very hard. You stay clean and fresh, and you don't have to worry about barking dogs, children on bicycles, or drivers who aren't paying attention to the road.

Even if I liked running, though, I wouldn't run. I was told several years ago I wasn't allowed to run. (Do you feel another story coming on?)

My sister, Shari, has twin girls. When Kellie and Laura were only a few months old, Shari and I took them with us as we shopped at one of the retail outlet centers in Lancaster. We parked my van near one end of the horseshoe-shaped row of stores, and began shopping in the first store in the row. We visited each store, one by one, as we made our way all the way around that horseshoe.

The girls were wonderful, but by the time we were wrapping up at the last store, they began to get fussy. Shari was in line to make a purchase, so I told her I'd take the girls to the van to get them in their car seats. By the time I was finished, she would probably be checked out of the store.

God Can Walk On His Eyeballs

So I took the girls, who were sitting in a side-by-side stroller, and I ran all the way across the parking lot. While I was running, they were so delighted! They giggled. They laughed. They squealed. Adorable!

When I got to the van, I was out of breath, I must confess. Suddenly, I thought I heard someone say my name. "Cindy." It was very distant and quiet, but I thought I heard it. I wondered, "Is that You, God?"

I looked all around the very busy parking lot. There were people everywhere, but none were calling my name that I could tell. I shrugged my shoulders, thinking I must have been hearing things and proceeded to unbuckle the babies from the stroller.

But I heard it again. "Cindy." It was louder now and sounded like it came from behind me. I turned around and looked even more carefully because this time, I know I heard my name. I spotted Shari, in the distance, just outside the last store we were in. She was cupping her hands around her mouth. She shouted to me again.

"Cindy," she hollered for the third time. (By this time, several people began to notice and were curiously watching this dialog take place.) I quieted the girls and cupped my hand behind my left ear so I was sure to hear her as clearly as possible. "It must be really important if she couldn't wait until she got to the van," I thought. "It's not like Shari to make a public spectacle of herself." She continued to call out this most important message.

"Don't run – ever again," she yelled. (And she flattened both of her hands and held them palms facing out, side by side, in the air, up in front of her face. She began to rapidly move each hand up and down, up and down, simulating motion.) And she finished yelling, "Your rear-end was doing this!"

I could have died! I could have killed her! She was laughing so hard, I think she was crying. She laughed all the way across the parking lot. By the time she got to the van, we were both laughing so hard we urgently needed to find a restroom!

To this day, I wonder about those other people in the parking lot. Who were they? What were they thinking? And of course, did they see my rear-end "doing this?" Oh my stars! You gotta love your sisters!

(In case you didn't notice, this sister is the one who asked me if she could write the foreword for this book. Of course, I was honored for her to do so, but a bit leery, as well. I would just like to point out here that Shari is much, much older than I am!)

Run? No, I don't run – ever again! I won't. I can't. I'm not allowed to! But in this passage in Hebrews 12, God's Word says we, as Christians, are running a race. When we received Jesus Christ as Savior, we were entered into the race of Christian life.

There are all kinds of runners, do you know that? Some runners are well-disciplined, they're focused and strong. They run like the wind!

Some runners like to sit on the sidelines and watch the other runners run by. They sip on their water bottles, and think, "Gee, that looks hard. Glad I'm not doing that!"

Other runners work very hard at the race, but somehow they seem to keep falling behind. It seems like the harder they run, the more they fall back. (Did you ever hear that Pennsylvania Dutch phrase, "The hurrier I go, the behinder I get?") These runners invented that phrase.

I call some runners the "running fools." They're just a runnin' and a smilin'- and they run their fool heads off. They're go to church all of the time and are involved in every single thing they get drawn into. They're juggling family life, church, work, and friends. They don't have one lick of sense about the direction that God has for their lives, however, because they're too busy - just a runnin' and a smilin'!

Regardless of the kind of runner you might tend to be, these verses give great instruction about how God says we are to run the race of this Christian life. Verse 1 paints a picture of a coliseum with many witnesses filling the surrounding seats. These are the believers who've already run their races. They're watching us run and cheering us on. Don't you just love that?

"You can do it, Cindy!"

"I know it's hard sometimes, but hang in there."

"I did it! You can, too!"

"It's so worth it! Press on!"

The rest of verse 1 tells us that in order to run the race with perseverance, in order to persevere to the end, we need to throw off everything that hinders, and throw off the sin that so easily entangles. While it might seem like these are the same, they are actually two different things.

Something that hinders a runner is anything that weighs him down. When this passage of scripture was written, runners threw off everything that might hinder them – they ran naked! (We're not even going there, girlfriend!)

Seriously, though, it's important to note that things that hinder us are not necessarily wrong, or bad, or sinful – in and of themselves. These tend to be things that keep us from putting forth our best effort. Things like television, phone calls (especially in today's world of cell phones, text messaging, and instant messaging), and computers.

Hindrances aren't just technological gadgets. Sometimes a hindrance can be a friend, or a group of friends, or shopping, or a good novel. These things are not necessarily sinful, but if we allow them to weigh us down – if they keep us from running the race set before us at our best - we are told to "throw them off." Throw them off so we can run more freely. So we are not weighed down. So we don't get weary before the race is over.

But the other thing we are to "throw off" paints a different picture – *"the sin that so easily entangles."*

Have you ever had a "blankie?" Or perhaps one of your children has or had a "blankie?"

Our son, Brandon, called his beloved blanket his "kiki." Now he's 21 years old and it's funny to look at this big, strapping young man who just "yesterday" cried his little eyes out waiting for that "kiki" to come out of the washing machine. He could barely make it through the time that it took for the dryer to do its job! He'd stand right in front of the machines prancing while he waited ever so impatiently.

Over the years, that blanket was nearly loved to death. And with years of washing and drying, the poor blanket ended up being a big old knot of yellow blanket strings – literally. My mother's heart wouldn't allow me to throw it away – because my baby boy loved that thing! So I saved it for him! It's in his "memory lane" box where I kept all of his unforgettable stuff over the years. Oh, how I wish you could have seen it in its last days. It is hideous! (I'm trying to think of ways to use it at his wedding rehearsal dinner or reception. Just kidding, Brandon and Lauren!)

In recent years, when we were moving to another home, Brandon came across his memory box. He opened it and pulled out the old knot of yellow strings, holding it with just the tips of his forefinger and thumb. As it dangled there, he looked at me and asked, "Mother, what is *this*?" (Unfortunately, I'm not sure how to describe the expression he had as he asked me this question. You'll just have to imagine one of confusion and revulsion. And you know when you're kids start off with "Mother," you're in trouble, right?)

I laughed and said, "Well, my son, *that* is your beloved "kiki.""

"*That,*" he replied, "is disgusting!" And he put it right back in his memory box! He still loves it, I know he does!

For years, Brandon had carried that blanket everywhere with him. It was usually draped over his shoulder, supported by one hand, while the other hand's thumb was in his mouth. Can't you just see him? Adorable! If he was sleepy, he wanted his "kiki." When he cried, only his "kiki" could comfort him properly.

Yet, that same precious, comforting "kiki" was the cause of so many stumbles and falls because Brandon was forever tripping over it! His little legs would get all wrapped up in it, as it twisted around his feet and through his legs. It "entangled" him. And all too often, he would fall down.

Do you get the picture here? "Sin that so easily entangles" is like a "kiki." Sin can be comforting at times, can't it? For awhile. Sin can feel good and warm, can't it? At least for a time. But the comfort, and the good, warm feelings of sin never last, because it's sin. It's completely against everything God is, and everything He stands for. Eventually, that warm, soft, cuddly blanket becomes a hard, ugly, smelly knot of yellow strings. It's disgusting!

"Sin that so easily entangles" will always trip you up. It will always cause you to fall. It will always cripple your race. Throw it off so you can run well!

Oh, there is so much "meat" in these few verses. The final point I wanted to share with you in this book is in verse 2.

"Let us fix our eyes on Jesus, the author and perfecter of our faith, who for the joy set before Him endured the cross, scorning its shame, and sat down at the right hand of the throne of God."

Just as a runner focuses on the finish line of a race, as followers of Christ, we are to focus on the very One who began and finished His race. Why might we be told to do this? To fix our eyes on Jesus? Because Jesus is the object and the goal of our faith, and because He is the perfect example of how to run it. To fix our eyes on Jesus means that we are to run this race with our eyes fixed only on Him, not on anyone or anything else.

Did you ever notice when you're driving your car down the road and you see something to the left or to the right? You look over and take your eyes off the road. I'm talking more than just glancing at it – you actually turn your head to the side to really look at it. As you're looking, what happens to your vehicle? You tend to turn the wheel in the direction you are looking, right?

It's the same principle here. When we fix our eyes on Jesus and stay mindfully focused on Him, guess what happens? We run right toward Him – THE Finish Line – the goal of our faith! Your Savior, my Savior, is there, at the finish line, waiting, watching, cheering us on.

And don't miss where Jesus was focused as He ran the race set before Him. Verse 2 - *"....who for the joy set before Him endured the cross, scorning its shame, and sat down at the right hand of the throne of God."*

According to this verse, why did Jesus endure the cross? Because of the joy set before Him. Do you realize what that joy is? It's you. It's me. We are His "joy" - the very reason He endured. The very reason He persevered. Then, when He completed His perfect work of redemption, He sat down at the right hand of God. "It is finished," He said.

And because of His example, we must remember that any of our present sufferings are far outweighed by our future joy. Life on this earth is temporary. Life in heaven is eternal, and we will be with Him in heaven for all eternity. (When we get there, if I haven't had the privilege of meeting you on this earth, would you please look me up in heaven? I'll be near the buffet, I'm sure. Most likely near the crab legs, just so you know.)

This race of Christian living isn't always an easy one - God never promised it would be. But I assure you, this race is *worth* it. Press on! The keys to running it well are so beautifully outlined in God's Word. I encourage you - I urge you - please dig in. He has so much to show you about how amazing He is!

Then, run, dear sister, run! Run,dear brother! Run like the wind! (I don't care what Shari says!)

Closing Thoughts

Every day is a new adventure with our God. You never know how He might reveal something about how truly amazing He is.

It may be through the person on the other end of the phone call you receive today – the friend who desperately needs your help. As you encourage her and pray for her, you'll notice His kind of love. Perhaps He'll show you how wonderful He is through your husband who works long days to ensure the family is well fed and warm at night. That's God's provision you're witnessing. Or maybe it's your children – the ones who make you so crazy. Yep, He's been known to use that signature move often. The child who's been trying your patience all day long - the child about whom you ask the daily question, "Why me, Lord?" This is the child who gestures for you to lean down and come closer to him so he can give you a kiss on your cheek. That's when you see God's amazing work of forgiveness and unconditional love. Sometimes it's when life throws its biggest curve balls that God's power and might are best revealed. You have no idea how you'll survive this trial. Look again.

It's in His arms you are resting. He's carrying you through to the other side.

People often tell me that I see God in everything – the daily grind, the problems I encounter, the great sale prices I find, the green lights in traffic, and even the red lights of life that stop me dead in my tracks. And I do see Him in all those places - I see Him because He's there! Right smack in the middle of my life, right where He wants to be, right where He belongs, right where *I* want Him to be. I've tried living this life my way and discovered I cannot do it.

His way is the only way I can experience true joy, peace, contentment, and freedom. And how wonderful it will be when I reach the end of my life and meet my Savior, Jesus Christ, face to face. Oh, how I want to hear Him say, "Well done, my good and faithful servant." Now, won't *that* be amazing?

Thanks for sharing some of your valuable time with me. Although you may have learned nothing new in the pages of my little book, I hope you were reminded of something you needed to hear. I hope you were encouraged. I hope you laughed. I hope you saw Him in each page. And as you reflect on Him – on His abilities, His love, His faithfulness, His holiness, His righteousness – I encourage you to open your eyes and look more closely. Squint your eyes of faith to see Him more clearly. He's right there, and He's got so many amazing things to show you, too!

"Call to me and I will answer you and tell you great and unsearchable things you do not know."

(Jeremiah 33:3 New International Version)